GROUP DYNAMICS

For Christian Counselors

Joseph J. Bohac, Ph.D.
and
Stan E. DeKoven, Ph.D.

GROUP DYNAMICS

For Christian Counselors

Joseph J. Bohac, Ph.D.

and

Stan E. DeKoven, Ph.D.

Copyright © 1995 BY JOSEPH J. BOHAC, PH.D.

2012 Second Edition with Stan DeKoven, Ph.D.

ISBN 978-1-61529-048-2

Vision Publishing
1672 Main St. E 109
Ramona, CA 92065
1-800-9-VISION
www.booksbyvision.com

All scripture references are taken from the New American Standard Version of the Bible unless otherwise noted.

ACKNOWLEDGMENTS

We wish to thank all of the wonderful people who have participated in Christian Growth Groups at Logos Christian Center. Much of the material in this volume is the outgrowth of those groups.

I want to especially thank Vision International University and Dr. Bohac, now home with the Lord, for his great work as a group leader, counselor, mentor and friend, and for his input to my life over many years.

Stan DeKoven

TABLE OF CONTENTS

INTRODUCTION

The concept of group counseling is not a new one. The earliest example can be found in the New Testament in the Book of Acts Chapter 2 where the first Christians usually met in small groups in someone's home. It has only been during the past decade or two that some of the modern day churches are beginning to see the need for such small groups, usually called home fellowship groups or cell groups.

Simply stated, group dynamics is the study of group behavior with special reference to the types of interactions that happen between and among persons in small groups involved in business and social activities. The beginning of the study of group dynamics in the psychological setting was first introduced in the U.S. by the social-psychologist Kurt Lewin.

The roots of group psychotherapy are undoubtedly in the science of sociology, or more correctly social-psychology. Sociology concerns itself with the interaction of groups of people, such as tribal groups, political groups, even large segments of a population as was the case in Nazi Germany at the beginning of World War II.

Social Psychology is that branch of psychology that is concerned with the scientific study of the behavior of individuals as influenced, directly or indirectly, by social stimuli. Social psychologists are interested in the thinking, emotions, desires, and judgment of individuals, as well as their overt behavior. The condition of an individual's inner state is inferred from some form of observable behavior. The Scripture says, "You brood of vipers, how can you, being evil, speak what is good? For the mouth speaks out of that which fills the heart." (Matthew 12:34). Yet another verse says, "For as he thinks within himself, so he is." (Proverbs 23:7).

Social psychology has its earliest beginnings in man's intellectual pursuits into his own relations with the rest of society. The early roots were to be found in the earlier studies and reasonings of the social philosophers such as Aristotle, Niccolo Machiavelli, Thomas Hobbes, and others throughout history. It is the application of scientific methods to the studies that brought about social psychology.

Primarily, social psychology is concerned with the way man interacts in groups and how that interaction is responsible for the formation of good social behavior or unacceptable social behavior. A social group can be anything from a small family to a large political party, or an entire nationality. Every group is made up of different kinds of people. The group is, however, more than just a group of people. There is a social-psychological dynamic that is in operation in even the smallest group that is as the gestalt would describe as being more than the sum total of each of the members of that group.

Long before the appearance of these philosophers, the Bible produced many insights into the relationships of men to other men. Indeed, it is those relationships that make up the course of man's existence on earth. Although God created man to have a relationship with Him, the journey that man must make towards that relationship with God is affected, to a great extent, by his relationship with other men also on that journey. Men that cannot live in harmony with their fellow men will never be able to find their way into relationship with God. The Word of God says, "If someone says, "I love God," and hates his brother, he is a liar; for the one who does not love his brother whom he has seen, cannot love God whom he has not seen." (1 John 4:20).

That part of social psychology that studies the phenomena of socialization, meaning the process of being made fit or trained for social environment, is focused on how individuals learn the rules governing their behavior toward one another in society. This aspect of the study of social psychology is believed to include how children learn languages, sex roles, moral and ethical principles, and appropriate behavior in general (Grumpert, et. al. in "Social psychology," Microsoft® Encarta Funk & Wagnall, 1993).

Attitudes and attitude change are also learned from one's interaction in social groups. How people feel about persons of different color, race, religion and cultural background is learned largely from the influences of other people in a person's family, school or other primary group. Often people within a group will develop attitudes toward other social classes of people as a primary result of needing to be accepted by their own group rather than basing their attitude on any other solid information. An example of this type of cultural prejudice can be found in the notorious influence of groups like the Klu Klux Klan. Fathers brought their sons into the organization, and over the years there developed a hatred of colored people in the younger people who did not wish to be considered "nigger lovers" by their peers and other members of the Klan.

Examples of cultural hatred can be found in all parts of the world. One nationality literally hates another without any concrete reason for their hatred. Often cultural hatred takes the form of cultural fears. These fears may be expressed in such outlandish expressions as, "All black men want to have sex with white women" or "Jews are only interested in getting all of the gentiles' money," and on, and on. One very successful method of changing cultural prejudice is through interaction in small groups.

It was also discovered through the study of small groups that participants are able to learn how to deal with different types of leadership. Later in this text, different types of leadership will be discussed. Some of the leadership types are less desirable than others. A more democratic leadership is, by far, the most successful in working with small groups in therapy. However, occasionally a member of the group will attempt to usurp leadership in the group and deal from a dictatorial position. Members of the group will have an opportunity, through interaction with the leader and other members of the group, to deal in a challenging, confrontational way with the new leader. Dealing with an aggressive, authoritative leader is learned in a much safer environment in the small group rather than in the everyday work place.

During this course of study, it will be seen that small groups can be of tremendous help for the individual members of the group. It is also true, that a rigorous and careful researcher can learn much about human psychology and social dynamics by observing groups in action. This second advantage of group dynamics is especially helpful in improving interpersonal relationship, to increase understanding of relations between members of groups in conflict with one another, and to diagnose and help correct problems in groups and organizational productivity. This could be a very helpful method for ministers to use in diagnosing and resolving conflicts within the church setting.

Other researchers, including William McDougall (1871-1938), because of his interest in human instincts, was concerned with the transmission of social behavior from person to person, such as the influence of one person's emotions on another's in a crowd (group) or the following of fads and fashions.

It was another American psychologist Floyd Allport, who had an important influence on the development of social psychology as a specialization of general psychology. Allport extended the principle of associative learning to account for a wide range of social behavior. The reasoning behind the type of work that Allport and others conducted was that man learned either good or bad behavior through the interaction he had with his primary group. It therefore stood to reason that in a controlled group which was designed to support acceptable behavior the unacceptable behavior could be changed. If the group influences negative or unacceptable behavior (anti-social), the group could also influence people to change their behavior to more socially acceptable forms. After Allport, the literature of social psychology continued to be devoted to observation with little empirical work of theoretical or practical significance being done.

It was in the early 1930's that the empirical research was undertaken on such matters as animal social behavior, group problem-solving attitudes and persuasion, national and ethnic stereotypes, rumor transmission, and leadership.

How the interest in groups as a form of psychotherapy developed is difficult to say. A number of individuals were developing theories over the past forty or fifty years. Much of the important concepts can probably be credited to the German-American psychologist Kurt Lewin (1890-1947). Lewin is considered the father of social psychology. He was greatly influenced by the Gestalt psychologists Wertheimer and Kafka.

In the year 1940, because he wanted to understand the behavior of groups, he finally established the Research Center for Group Dynamics. Work at the center led to the establishment of the National Training Laboratories at Bethel, Maine, where the T-Group (short for training groups) approach to interpersonal skills training was born (more on T-groups later).

An important study was conducted and published in 1939 in which Lewin and his students reported the results of an experiment on leadership roles. The researchers had the same adults play different leadership roles while directing matched groups of children. The adults attempted to establish particular climates, that is, social environmental conditions of democratic, autocratic, or completely laissez-faire leadership. The reactions of the children in the groups were carefully observed, and detailed notes were taken on the patterns of social interaction that emerged. Although the experiment itself had many deficiencies, it demonstrated that something as nebulous as a democratic social climate could be created under controlled laboratory conditions. (Encarta *Social Psychology*, Funk and Wagnall, 1993).

Another important beginning of interest in group dynamics can be traced back before the work of Lewin, to Triplett's (1898) studies of how the mere presence of others may influence an individual's performance. Triplett conducted one of social psychology's first experiments. He reported that children would string (an instrument) faster when they worked with others rather than when they performed alone. Although, not all studies produced the same results, these early studies peaked the curiosity of other researches in social psychology.

A renewed interest in groups came as a result of some observations made by certain psychologists during the bombings of London during World War II. Each evening, as the bombs and the V2 rockets began to rain on London, the people would hurry to the bomb shelters underground. Once relatively safe in the shelters, they would tend to cluster into small groups of 10-15 people. Over time, these groups would become rather permanent in structure, and the people began sharing their personal fears, family concerns, etc., although most of them were not personal acquaintances in everyday life when the blitz was not on. Observers of these small groups were impressed with one important fact: in addition to the encouragement of social interaction that relieved some of the tenor of the nightly bombings, individuals in these groups seemed to gain some genuine help and healing as a result of the interaction of the members of the group.

Years after the war was over, some of the psychologists that experienced those horrible days in England began to theorize about what happened to the people in the shelters. As a result of those studies a proliferation of different kinds of groups and the whole concept of group dynamics began.

There were many different types of group therapies that were spawned. Someone has estimated that there were about seventeen different types of groups developed (Liebermann, et. al., 1973). A few of the groups that gained more attention than others are the following:

1. Task Groups
2. Counseling Groups
3. Fellowship Groups
4. Training Groups (T-Groups)
5. Encounter Groups

6. Therapy Groups

7. Marathon Groups

8. Care Groups

9. Restoration Groups (Recovery)

10. Sensory Awareness Group

11. Christian Growth Groups

Group behavior affects many different aspects of life. Group dynamics is concerned with the structure and functioning of groups with the types of roles played by members. Roles are flexible and may change with changing goals, activities, or style of leadership. The study of group dynamics is important in order to understand and facilitate productivity, and in the case of therapy groups, [promote] healing (Encarta, 1993. Funk and Wagnall's Corporation).

Following is a brief summary of each of the above 11 group types (these groups will be covered in greater detail in Chapter 1).

A. Task Groups: A group that is formed to accomplish a specific task. This could include the church committee to select the carpeting for the new sanctuary or the committee to purchase a new church organ. Many churches have a "pulpit committee" whose task is to select a minister for consideration as the church's new pastor. The important consideration with regard to task groups is that each member should be selected carefully on the basis of their qualifications and their ability to focus on the specific task of the group. An individual that is totally tone deaf might not be able to contribute much in a positive way to the organ selection committee.

B. Counseling Groups: The primary function of this type of group is to meet the needs of the members of the group. There are many important advantages to the use of counseling groups in the church milieu. Most pastors are not physically able to meet and counsel with every individual in the church that may have some emotional or interrelational problems. The counseling group can take much of the burden of this need off of the pastor. The most important considerations in the use of counseling groups are the qualifications and spiritual, emotional stability of the leader of such a group. Care must also be used in the selection of the persons who will participate in the group. Severely disturbed individuals and certain borderline personalities are best left to the professional counselor on a one to one basis.

C. Fellowship Groups: This type of group is designed to meet the needs of people who are basically well-adjusted individuals in need of a more specialized type of fellowship. These groups might include: Widows groups, Singles groups, Military wives groups, new converts group, etc. This list can be very long.

D. Training Groups (T-Groups): As the name implies, this type of group has as a goal training. T-Groups are used to train management level personnel to learn how to more effectively deal with personnel problems in the work place. A T-Group may be formed to help teachers and staff work more effectively in a multicultural neighborhood school. Police may be trained to handle gang situations more effectively through training in a T-Group. The T-Group differs from a regular classroom setting in which a teacher instructs participants in effective methods of doing things. The group allows members to share in the teaching process and deal with specific problems that they face each day.

E. Encounter Groups: The encounter group became very popular in the 60's and 70's. There were many variations on this type. The Western Behavioral Sciences Institute in La Jolla, California, was one of the leading proponents of this type of therapy group. Gestalt psychologists also found that the encounter group was an effective method of "getting in touch with feelings."

F. Therapy Groups: Therapy groups are groups that are held in a hospital setting under the leadership of a psychiatrist or a clinical psychologist specially trained in therapy type groups.

Participants in these types of groups are usually moderately to seriously borderline personality types. They are often confined to the hospital and under medication for their disorder. This is not to say that therapeutic healing cannot take place in other types of groups. Actually, many people experience healing, emotional, spiritual, and physical, in various kinds of groups. This is especially true in the Care Groups that are becoming very popular in churches throughout the world.

G. Marathon Groups: Counseling groups and Christian growth groups work well in the marathon mode. The main advantage of the Marathon Group is that of breaking down defenses. The Marathon Group meets for a long period of time in one meeting (Friday 7-12, Saturday 8am-10pm and Sunday 8am-4 or 5pm). It has been demonstrated by research that the group will begin to let down their defenses as they become weary several hours into group. The Marathon Group, as well as some of the others, will use certain games such as role playing, hot seat, etc., to help the group get started. Christian Growth Groups, and many of the other counseling groups, do not look favorably on the use of games.

H. Care Groups: Care groups take on many different forms. The past few years has brought on the age of the mega church. Churches with membership of 5000 and more are becoming more common. One of the things that happened with the advent of the mega church is that pastors and leaders realized that there was a large diversity and complexity of needs represented by the large number of people. Pastors recognized that the church needed to make provision for meeting those needs in new and innovative ways. One of the methods that the larger churches adopted was the **"Cell Group Ministry."** Smaller churches had for years been involved in counseling groups, but for a different reason.

I. Recovery Groups: Mainly deriving from the original concepts of Alcoholics Anonymous and their 12 Step concept, recovery groups are prevalent around the   world, although not without controversy in the Christian community, have been most helpful and successful in assisting men and women by the thousands achieve sobriety. These may include: recovering alcoholics, drug addicts, homosexuals, adult children of alcoholics, abusive parents, victims of abuse (sexual, physical, etc.), overeaters, anorexics, and on and on the list may go.

For a number of years after the first Christian Growth Groups began to appear in churches around the country, many of the old line fundamentalist pastors denounced them as being worldly (because of the use of some psychological terminology), or down right demonic. A few of the more outspoken preachers may have actually avoided their fall into disgrace, if they had been able to be in one of those early groups. Pastors and other Christian workers are often reluctant to become involved in a group for fear that someone may discover their basic faults. Unfortunately, pastors and TV evangelists are as susceptible to the same emotional, mental, spiritual and physical defects as everyone else. Few church denominations provide any kind of counseling or support for pastors and Christian workers. This is why so many become a victim of serious problems that often destroy their ministries, as well as, the lives of those who followed them.

The larger churches began developing cell groups patterned after the ministry of David Younggi Cho in Korea. However; in order to meet the specialized need of many of the people in the larger churches, pastors began developing specialized types of groups. Some of the many different types are:

God and Government CARE Group: This group meets periodically to discuss the Christian's role in politics from a biblical perspective.

Hispanic CARE Groups: Especially in certain large metropolitan areas, Hispanics often develop unique kinds of emotional, economic, and health problems that can be helped through the CARE group ministry.

CARE Groups for the Hearing Impaired: Because of the unique needs of the hearing impaired, for meaningful relationships and fellowship, the CARE group ministry is well suited to help meet those needs.

Singles' CARE Groups: Here again is a special group of people with special needs.

Young Marrieds' CARE Groups: Young people are seldom prepared for the special kinds of relational problems that occur in marriage. Premarital counseling is a great help in preparing young people for the "great step," but often two young people in love, seldom take seriously enough the admonitions of their pastor before marriage.

Youth CARE Groups: With all of the pressures on young people in modem society, there is a great need to minister to them in the small group situation. Large youth rallies are fine and have a place in the ministry of the church, but individual needs are seldom met or even addressed in such rallies.

Children's' CARE Groups: These groups may take on many forms. There may be groups for children from abusive homes, groups for children with special physical limitations, etc. The prospects are as unlimited as the imagination.

Seniors' CARE Groups: Seniors often feel left out of the mainstream of the church's activities. Most churches, especially the larger ones, are youth oriented and seniors must simply sit around on the fringes and observe. The greatest need for Christian CARE is with the seniors who are left behind through the death (or divorce) of a mate.

The name of the group isn't as important as the need that it addresses. One of the needs of every church is to ascertain what the needs of the congregation are and to develop ministries to meet those needs. Also, in the study of group dynamics, it is not the value or lack of value of a particular type of group that is important. The focus of attention is what happens to people in these groups. It is a question of how people interact in the presence of other people and under different types of leadership.

Evangelism:

One of the benefits of the group ministries that really surprises many pastors is that, when a church begins offering CARE group ministries, the word will soon get around the community, and before long, people who may never come to the church for any other reason will come to one of the groups being offered by the church. It is reasonable to believe, that once these unchurched people discover the healing power of the Christian environment, they will almost certainly become involved in the other activities, such as the worship services.

When a church develops a counseling center as a part of the church ministry, they almost always begin to see new people coming to the church.

Recovery Groups: Although we mentioned the recovery group as one kind of care group, there are many different types of these groups already mentioned above.

J. Sensory Awareness Groups: This type of group is relatively new. The goals of the technique are to help members become more aware of sensory experiences as well as to discover the effects of sensory deprivation (The Colossus Ride at Magic Mountain theme park in California, is an example of sensory awareness).

K. Christian Growth Groups: The Christian Growth Group does not appear on the chart of groups, because this type of group activity did not begin until the middle seventies and was primarily a function of the church. A number of Christian group styles began developing in the early 1970's. One such was the **Yokefellow's** founded by **Cecil Osborn** in Burlingame California, This group technique involved the use of the **Minnesota Multiphasic Personality Inventory (MMPI)** and the **DAP (Draw A Person)** as a guide to help group members uncover areas of their personality that needed healing or simple change. The groups met for about thirteen weeks, and every other week each member of the group received an evaluation slip to share with the group.

The Yokefellow's organization developed many other tests that could be used in a similar fashion such as a **Married Couples Test, A Youth Inventory, etc.**

Bruce Larson and other Christian leaders developed their own **"Adventures In Christian Living" groups. Keith Miller** wrote a book and produced an audio tape that was used to guide group members through various exercises (adventures) in Christian growth.

The Christian Growth Groups as they came to be known at Logos Christian Center in San Diego, California under the leadership of this author, were somewhat like the encounter groups mentioned earlier, except that these groups were not as confrontive, but were tempered with Christian love and compassion. The Christian Growth Group would come under the classification of Counseling **Group**. The goal of the counseling Group and the Christian Growth Group is basically the same: healing that will facilitate spiritual growth.

Yalom (1975) in his research with group counseling concluded that there were eleven "common elements" or "curative factors," and he divided them into the following categories:

1. Instillation of hope — the creation of a sense of optimism and positive expectations. Soren Kierkegaard (1813-1855) a Danish Christian wrote about the loss of hope as the "sickness unto death."

2. Universality — decreasing each member's sense of being alone in his misery and psychopathology. Although there are many people who really enjoy their solitude, most people need and cherish the company of other humans, especially in times of sorrow or fear such as was noted in the bombing of London during WWII.

3. Imparting of information about mental health and illness-Many people, at one time or another, will think of themselves as being "different" or "not quite right." The group can help people to discover that most people are experiencing the same kinds of fears, doubts, and anxieties. The old adage "misery loves company" is a variation of this concept. It is not that people love to be around others who are miserable but rather people take great comfort from the fact that all humans are in some way in the same boat, rowing upstream!

4. Altruism — the creation of a group climate of helpfulness, concern, support and sharing. The opportunity to help someone else, who is suffering in some way, is a sure tonic for the one who can "lend a helping hand."

5. Corrective recapitulation (reconstruction, reconstitution) of the primary family group — helping group members to see that their interactions in the group recapitulate with primary family members.

6. Development of socializing techniques — increasing group members' ability to relate to one another in positive and mature ways within a safe environment. In the group, a member can be confrontive without fear of being fired from his job or divorced by his wife.

7. Imitative Behavior — helping group members change via observation and imitation of functional, mature behavior on the part of the therapist and other group members. Participation in a group can help individuals discover parts of their basic personality that is out of line with what is acceptable in society. Groups can help individuals change.

8. Interpersonal learning— utilizing transference, corrective emotional experience, and insight to assist members in changing themselves.

9. Cohesiveness — the sense of togetherness that causes a group to see itself holistically rather than as a collection of individuals.

10. Catharsis — the open expression of affect, within the group process. Catharsis has to do with an emotional purgation. It refers to a release of negative feeling in a positive way.

11. Existential factors — dealing with such issues as personal responsibility, contingency, basic isolation and mortality.

A CASE IN POINT

A case could be made that Jesus himself demonstrated the full usage of the basic principles of group dynamics (as outlined by Yalom) in His final meeting with the disciples, just prior to His death, on the night of the Passover meal. Christians celebrate the Passover meal every time they eat the bread and drink the cup of the New Covenant. In John Chapter 13, Jesus is seen putting into motion several different aspects of this principle. The aspect of Altruism can be seen in His creation of the group climate of helpfulness, concern, support and sharing.

The development of socializing techniques can be seen as Jesus increased their ability to relate to one another in a positive and mature form of servant hood, all within a safe protected "upper room" environment.

Imitative behavior was developed when each of the disciples, in turn, followed the Lord's example of humility when He stripped down and washed their dirty feet. Now, think about that for a minute - roads were very dirty in that day. Not only were they dirty, but the animals pulled carts and were ridden down the same roads that the people walked down.

Cohesiveness or the sense of togetherness was developed when the disciples learned that they were responsible for cleaning up their fellow disciples' uncleanness. "Your mess is my mess, what must I do to help?" Or "The care of your body is my responsibility, for we are truly one Body in Christ"

The insights developed could readily be seen as Interpersonal Learning.

Although it is not reported directly in this passage, more than likely, there was some catharsis that took place. It is not too difficult to picture the Creator of Heaven and Earth, the Lord of Glory, down on His hands and knees before His precious, but soiled creation, the sons of men, or mankind.

It is not too difficult either to imagine how the disciples must have felt when they saw the Lord bowed down before them, washing the filth of their daily walk from their feet. It is easier to understand Peter's reaction, and then one can actually take the time to visualize what truly occurred.

Installation of hope occurred for the disciples when each of them saw that their needs would be cared for by the group. "If I fail, someone will be there to clean me up, and help me get better," would be the thought of the heart at a time like this. The student should be able to clearly identify these elements in this passage taken from John 13:4-14.

"Jesus got up from supper, and laid aside His garments; and taking a towel, He girded Himself. Then He poured water into the basin, and began to wash the disciples' feet and to wipe them with the towel with which He was girded. So He came to Simon Peter. He said to Him, "Lord, do You wash my feet?" Jesus answered and said to him, "What I do you do not realize now, but you will understand hereafter." Peter said to Him, "Never shall You wash my feet!" Jesus answered him, "If I do not wash you, you have no part with Me." Simon Peter said to Him, "Lord, *then wash* not only my feet, but also my hands and my head." Jesus said to him, "He who has bathed needs only to wash his feet, but is completely clean; and you are clean, but not all *of you*." For He knew the one who was betraying Him; for this reason He said, "Not all of you are clean." So when He had washed their feet, and taken His garments and reclined *at the table* again, He said to them, "Do you know what I have done to you? You call Me Teacher and Lord; and you are right, for *so* I am. If I then, the Lord and the Teacher, washed your feet, you also ought to wash one another's feet."

Jesus said that Christians are to walk in love, just as Christ also loved you and gave Himself up for us, an offering and a sacrifice to God as a fragrant aroma. (Ephesians 5:2). Christians are to imitate the patterns that Jesus demonstrated in service to God and one another.

Later on the very same night, Jesus dealt with other issues in ways that can be identified in terms of Group Dynamics. When He taught the disciples about His going to the Father and sending the Comforter He instilled hope. He imparted information about their mental health when He prepared them for the onslaught of criticism they would reap for being His disciples. He let them know they were not alone in their future suffering or glory to come. Existential factors were dealt with when He relayed to them His impending crucifixion and glorious resurrection. A thorough reading of John Chapters 13-17 will reveal this and much more to the student, concerning proper use and application of Group Dynamics. It has been said that the only more powerful group session that has ever been experienced, was the one that occurred in this very same room (according to many scholars) a few weeks later. It begins with, *"And when the day of Pentecost was fully come..."* And the rest is history.

This is not to imply that Jesus must have studied psychology somewhere and subsequently used it on His disciples. What this does imply is that Jesus, who was and is God in human form, is the creator of the human psyche. He fully knew the hearts and minds of His disciples. He knew what they needed because He was and still is the Creator of all. As such, He fully demonstrated the very principles of group dynamics in His dealings with men. Christian counselors should use them today in effective counseling. Maybe if more of His methods were used, counselors could expect more of His kind of results!

Meier, Paul D. et. al. (1991) suggests that one of the major functions of groups is that they provide people with the opportunity to practice communicating accurately with each other. These authors present some very important insights regarding small group activities. Actually, small groups have been with the church for a long time in the form of board meetings, Sunday school, etc. Earlier examples include the home meetings of Wesley's time. The use of small groups as a means of healing or therapy is relatively new to the church. One of the advantages of small groups, according to Meier, includes the effectiveness of the small group in dealing with interpersonal problems. The interpersonal factor is what Yalom called the socializing factor. Meier also suggests that efficiency is a major justification of small group ministries.

BIBLICAL PERSPECTIVE

Although little can be found in the Bible dealing directly with the concept of group counseling (because the Bible was not written as a book on psychotherapy), it is not too difficult to come to the conclusion that because of the importance of human relationships, the use of group counseling can be of inestimable value. Such human problems such as feelings of isolation, broken relationships, self-esteem issues, and many areas of compulsive behavior that tend to generate great guilt, can conceivably be best handled in the group setting.

It should also be noted that in the early church, the Christians met in small home groups. They did not have large churches to attend, although in the very beginning the early disciples continued to attend the synagogue. With all that is written in the New Testament (especially in the Book of Ephesians) about body ministry, and the practice encouraged by the Apostle Paul for every member of the body to have something to do when they met together, the house meetings of the early church must have closely resembled Christian Growth Groups.

In 1 Corinthians 14:26 it is recorded, "What is *the outcome* then, brethren? When you assemble, each one has a psalm, has a teaching, has a revelation, has a tongue, has an interpretation. Let all things be done for edification." This type of activity would hardly be possible in the larger churches of modern Christendom.

In James 5:16, Christians are encouraged to, "Therefore, confess your sins to one another, and pray for one another so that you may be healed. The effective prayer of a righteous man can accomplish much..." Again this suggests that the meetings were small in the number of people in attendance.

Other biblical examples of small group ministry certainly include Jesus' first concern for his small group of disciples, as shown in John 13:24-35, and 17:22-23. The twelve disciples passed that tradition onto the first century church.

John 13:24-35 (NW) "Simon Peter motioned to this disciple and said, "Ask him which one he means." Leaning back against Jesus, he asked him, "Lord, who is it?" Jesus answered, 'it is the one to whom I will give this piece of bread when I have dipped it in the dish." Then, dipping the piece of bread, he gave it to Judas Iscariot, son of Simon. As soon as Judas took the bread, Satan entered into him. "What you are about to do, do quickly," Jesus told him, but no one at the meal understood why Jesus said this to him. Since Judas had charge of the money, some thought Jesus was telling him to buy what was needed for the Feast, or to give something to the poor. As soon as Judas had taken the bread, he went out. And it was night. When he was gone, Jesus said, 'Now is the Son of Man glorified and God is glorified in him. If God is glorified in him, God will glorify the Son in himself and will glorify him at once. "My children, I wilt be with you only a little longer. You will look for me, and just as I told the Jews, so I tell you now: Where I am going, you cannot come "A new command I give you: Love one another As I have loved you, so you must love one another By this all men will know that you are my disciples, if you love one another"

"And the glory which thou gavest me I have given them; that they may be one, even as we are one: I in them, and thou in me, that they may be perfect in one; and that the world may know that thou hast sent me, and hast loved them, as thou hast loved me," (John 17:22-23).

Meier (1991) suggests that Christians can get better feedback for better self-understanding from the small Christian group than from the world. He suggests that Romans 12:3 warns, "Not to think of himself more highly than he ought to think, but rather to think soberly according as God hath dealt to every man the measure of faith." This can best be accomplished, says Meier in the "context of the Body of Christ and of the gifts given to members.' Meier also points out that Galatians 6:3 reminds us that it is easy for Christians to deceive themselves, and that, in the group context, an accurate self-identity can be facilitated through interpersonal interaction

Meier (pp 323) further posts that Philippians 2:4 and Galatians 6:2 are both an excellent scriptural basis for group interaction among Christians "Look not every man on his own things, but every man also on the things of others," (Philippians 2:4) "Bear ye one another's burdens and so fulfill the law of Christ," (Galatians 6:2).

Small groups afford an opportunity to accurately know and understand the needs of others and to minister to those needs in a much more empathic way. Most people do not need others to feel sorry (sympathy) for them, but they do need people to feel with them (empathy). People with real burdens are seldom helped through broadcast type of ministry. It takes the personal intimate interpersonal interaction to understand and wisely minister to most of the burdens being carried by a large number of Christians.

"Like one who takes away a garment on a cold day, or like vinegar poured on soda, is one who sings songs to a heavy heart," (Proverbs 25:20, NIV).

During the 1980's, the small group movement grew very rapidly. This was especially true as religious leaders began to recognize the potential of such groups as a way of bringing new vitality into congregations that were beginning to slowly decline (Wuthnow, 1994). Many researchers foresee a continued growth in the 1990's. The use of groups is to be found among the Catholic parishes, the Jewish communities, as well as in the Protestant churches.

According to a survey conducted by Wuthnow, 40% of the

population of the United States, (18 years and over), claim to be involved in small groups. The survey revealed that 38% of the population was involved in two or three groups. With these and other findings of the survey, it can be estimated that currently in the United States there are approximately 3 million small groups operating. This figure does not include children or teenagers under 18-years-old.

Many of the groups represented in the survey by Wuthnow were not necessarily therapy groups, but as this text will posit, almost any good group will have a therapeutic character to it. Although more will be said regarding group leaders later, it is important to note at this juncture, that a group is only as good as the leadership of the group.

In home Bible study groups, or the therapy and care groups listed above, the most important element is **Trained Group leaders**.

Yalom (1975) also reports on the responses to a questionnaire sent to a large number of individuals who had been in groups of various types. The respondents listed the following as values of the group experience:

1. Increased awareness of emotional dynamics: The subjects were helped to acquire new knowledge about themselves, their strengths and weaknesses, patterns of interpersonal relating, motivations, etc.

2. Recognizing similarity to others: This is the "We are all in the same boat" simile of life as a human being.

3. Feeling positive regard, acceptance, and sympathy for others: Some people are so involved in their own problems that they seldom, if ever, take the time to feel for others. This is also called self-centeredness, or egoism.

4. Seeing self as seen by others: Often people think that people see them in a certain (often negative) way, and they are surprised to discover that their perception of how others see them is incorrect. It has been said that the rest of the group members

serve as a mirror to the member who is sharing.

5. Expressing self congruently, articulately, or assertively in the group: In some societies more than others, children are taught overtly or by implication that they should, "be seen, but not heard." It is not uncommon for individuals to grow up feeling that it is not polite or civilized to be assertive. In most dysfunctional families, children learn to hide their true feelings, and in time, are not able to express either positive or negative feelings openly. Children in dysfunctional families also grow up learning to say what they think they are expected to say. A good group experience can be helpful in opening the doors to true self-expression.

6. Witnessing honesty, courage, openness, or expressions of emotionality in others: Women are often amazed to discover how much sensitivity most men really have.

7. Feeling responded to by others: In most groups, members will be very surprised to realize that others are really listening to them. They have spent most of their lives feeling that "no one ever listens, or pays any attention to what I say?"

8. Feeling warmth and closeness generally in the group: Although many groups will have a rather rocky beginning, almost all groups will end with the members feeling a genuine kinship and love for one another.

9. Ventilating Emotions: (Also referred to as catharsis).

This text was developed to provide the individuals who were interested in preparing themselves for a ministry in the field of Christian Counseling. Although the academic information is of great importance, it is imperative to note that the only way an individual can develop the required skills for conducting effective Christian groups of any kind, is to be actively involved in groups of various kinds, both as a participant and especially as a group leader. The mastery of the contents of this volume will only result in effective ministry if the student is involved in a practicum as a group facilitator (the concept of what is required in a good group facilitator will be covered in the chapter dealing with group leadership).

We (both Dr. Bohac and Dr. DeKoven) first became interested in groups as a part of my doctoral courses at U.S. International University. The University had a close relationship with the Western Behavioral Sciences Institute in La Jolla where Dr. Carl Rogers worked. As a part of the core courses required in my (Dr. Bohac) program, we each had to act as a facilitator for several different groups. These early groups were much like the earlier encounter groups.

The groups met for four hours on Friday evening, ten hours on Saturday, and four to six hours on Sunday. In this respect, they were Marathon Groups. In spite of the fact the Carl Rogers was considered a Humanist (more by others than by his own admission); I found working with him to be very stimulating and educational. He never "acted" as if he was a humanist, but he had an obvious love for mankind. The experience I received in these groups made me aware of the great potential for groups in the church.

After I (Dr. Bohac) finished my doctorate at USIU, and Dr. DeKoven completed his at the Professional School for Psychological Studies, we became acquainted with the Burlingame Counseling Center in Burlingame, California... Cecil Osborn, a retired Baptist minister, started the counseling center and developed the concept of group counseling as a result of his book, The Art of Understanding Yourself. So many people became interested in the therapy that was suggested in the book in the form of Yokefellow Groups, that the center soon began offering groups almost every week. In time, Dr. Osborn developed a training program for potential Yokefellow Group leaders. I was privileged to attend a number of those workshops.

Some of the people in the small church I (Dr. Bohac, Dr. DeKoven was a member, one of the first members) pastored in San Diego also became interested in training as leaders. Before long, we had a number of what became known as Christian Growth Groups meeting at our fellowship. The good that came from those groups can never be completely told, but from time to time in the text, I shall record some of the more outstanding healings and some of the examples of group dynamics in operation.

Many see the small group phenomenon as evidence of the fact that people in general are beginning to feel a real need for a return to the Christian concept of community. Some of the current literature calls for a return to community as a way of life. Authors like M. Scott Peck have been calling the world to an awareness of the need for community. In his *A World Waiting to Be Born*, Peck builds a strong case for the need for a return to civility. He maintains that civility can only come through group consciousness. The process of regaining a sense of civility starts with restoring relationship in the family, in the work place, in the world.

What is it about the small group that encourages people to be more active in community activities? Community here does not refer only to the civic community, but to the religious community that is the Body of Christ.

However, it has been demonstrated that people who are involved in small groups tend to be more actively involved in the community as a whole. Wuthnow (1994) suggests that the following are all among the possibilities:

- People in groups have been raised with more religion and therefore, caring values in the first place.

- People in small fellowship groups are exposed to needs and opportunities for volunteer service because they belong to churches.

- People in small fellowship groups take their faith more seriously, so they are more interested in serving others.

- People in small fellowship groups have experienced God's love more deeply, so they desire to show this love to others.

- People in small fellowship groups come into contact with other people, are more people-oriented, and learn about opportunities to serve in other ways.

Wuthnow's research also concluded the following points that underscore the value of group ministry within the church community:

1. Forty percent of the American public is currently involved in some kind of small group.

2. The people who are involved in small groups are not terribly different from those who are not involved. They come from all walks of life and are thus representative of a vast majority of the rest of society.

3. Small groups in American society are enormously diverse. The focus on different issues, follow different formats, vary in how they are organized, and draw people together from a wide variety of backgrounds.

4. At the same time, small groups are fairly stable and are taken quite seriously by most of their members. Small groups are not a novelty to be "tried for a possible activity to keep people out of trouble?"

5. Small groups provide encouragement and a wide variety of other services to most of their members. People who participate regularly seem to be highly satisfied with their group.

6. It does not take a great deal of special knowledge or skill to make a small group function well. There is a surplus of literature dealing with groups and how to lead them, but many believe that for most groups, a minimum of training is necessary.

7. Small groups do not, for the most part, compromise the individuality of their members.

8. Many small-group members feel spiritually nurtured by their groups. This is the feeling of community, of belonging.

The rest of this text will be organized as follows: Chapter One will deal with the topic of the different types of groups. Chapter Two will present the dynamics of group interaction. Chapter Three will present an in-depth discussion of the qualities of a good leader (facilitator). This chapter will also deal with the problems that may occur as a result of a leader with certain unresolved issues in his or her own life. Chapter Four will present some ways of starting a group. Chapter Five will focus on some techniques that can be used in groups. Chapter Six will discuss methods of evaluating group success. Chapter Seven will be a summary of the entire book.

Note:

There are many fine books on group counseling, a few of which are listed in the Bibliography. In the previous edition of this work, Dr. Bohac referred to my (Dr. DeKoven) book, 12 Steps to Wholeness, which has now been incorporated into this book.

"… when the whole group is together, each brining out all that is best, wisest, or funniest in all the others. Those are the golden sessions when the whole world, and something beyond the world, opens itself to our minds as we talk and no one has any claim on or any responsibility for another, but all are freedmen and equals as if we had first met an hour ago, while at the same time an Affection mellowed by the years enfolds us. Life- natural life- has no better gift to give." C.S. Lewis -

CHAPTER 1:

TYPES OF GROUPS

What is a group? Most social psychologists would agree that a group is not a mere collection of people; rather, a true group involves people whose behavior is to some extent interdependent and who recognize a degree of mutual relationship (Schnieder, 1988). By interdependence social-psychologists mean that each person in the group influences others. The concept of group as used in psychotherapy and counseling fits fairly well with this definition, although the counseling group usually begins as a group of strangers, or at least individuals that are not otherwise in any particular social grouping. From the point of view of the sociologist, the family, even a husband and wife, constitutes a group. In the case of the family as a model, it can be seen that the group (family) is more than the sum of the two people involved. Something wonderful, yet difficult to understand, happens as a result of the interaction of two people in a relationship. When children enter the picture the dynamics become even more complex.

Once a counseling group is organized, the individuals tend to become a group in the sense of the definition offered by social psychologists and although each individual does not lose his or her own sense of person, the group experience will result in the individual discovering more about himself or herself than they ever knew before.

Most of the early scientific research into the interaction of groups was conducted by the social psychologists. In more recent years, with the advent of the various psychological groups such as the sensitivity groups, etc., some very serious and interesting research has been conducted by the field of psychology. It was the social psychologists who were responsible for bringing much of the respectability to the field of psychology. This is especially true of the work of Kurt Lewin mentioned earlier.

Humans are social animals. They have a need to interact relationally with other humans. The loner or hermit is not considered by psychology as emotionally healthy. This does not mean to imply that persons who may enjoy solitude and times of reflection and meditation are not healthy. Individuals who do not enjoy any contact with other humans are usually diagnosed as being sociopathic, as Ruben Welch expressed in his fine book, *We Really Do Need Each Other.*

Social psychologists would contrast the concept of group with other collections of people such as aggregates of people defined by geographical, gender, racial, or demographic characteristics (Schnieder, 1988, p. 275). The term group in this text refers to a specific group of individuals gathered together for a specific task. That task may be to formulate a new policy regarding the type of music to be used in worship at a church, a committee to select a new pastor, a committee to purchase a new church organ, or in the case of the content of this book, a group of individuals gathered together to interact on a personal relationship basis in order to deal with interpersonal and personal problems.

Most of man's problems revolve around his or her personal relationship with others. This relationship problem may be in the work situation or on a much more crucial level with persons that are significant others, (lovers, husbands, wives, parents, etc.). It is generally believed by psychologists (and social psychologists), that men can learn the all-important personal emotional skills necessary to interact with those people close to them best by interacting with people not so closely related to them in a well-organized psychological group.

Groups do serve other functions. In the case of care groups, individuals may learn to deal with the emotional struggles of grief, physical pain, alcohol, drug and other addictive behavior. This text will endeavor to deal at least briefly with most of the different types of groups. The major emphasis, however, will be the Christian Growth Group, and other Christian Counseling Groups. The same dynamics apply to all of the different types of groups.

The group as defined thus far is definitely different than an aggregate of people. The group as used in this sense is intended to result in interaction between people. That interaction is what has become known as **Group Dynamics.** A group in which the members are interactive will experience change and adjustment in their feelings, beliefs and hopefully their behavior. This is what is meant by **Group Dynamics**.

Bonner (1959) notes an interesting observation regarding the dynamics of groups. The term collective determinism was suggested by Emile Durkheim (1898) and others who suggested that the concept that the whole is not composed of the sum of its parts; it includes them but also differs from them. He went on to say that, "while collective representations are composed of individual representations, the collective representations are at the same time distant from them." This is Durkheim's way of saying that although each member of the group in unique and individual, when in the group situation and in interaction with others, the same individual becomes more through that interaction.

There is a dynamic at work that alters in some ways the significance of certain feelings and emotions in the individual. Psychology has shown that certain individuals can function at a certain level in solitude, while in the presence of others especially when interaction is required, their level of functioning changes. This is one suggested support for group counseling. A perspective of an individual may change considerably in the group-situation.

In one of the groups I led, there was a woman in her mid-fifties who seemed to be very "spiritual" and completely devoted to the Lord Jesus Christ. Her speech and demeanor suggested a devout Christian, whose only real goal in life was to "serve the Lord in every way possible."

In one of the early meetings, Helen (not her real name) shared the following: "I can hardly wait to get home from work and lie on my bed and make love to my Lord." Several of the other members of the group found this statement a little annoying and contrived. As the group progressed through the evening, Helen finally shared the following. "I can't understand how the Lord can love so much and at the same time follow me around with a big stick waiting to bash me if I do anything wrong." Helen was obviously a victim of a very strict legalistic church in which she had been taught the awful severity of God. We were not able to help Helen very much. She obviously needed a great deal of personal counseling to be healed of the terrible spiritual abuse she had suffered since childhood in a church that did not believe or teach the concept of a loving Father.

A **good group** is one that has the following qualities:

1. Cohesiveness-This is what Griffin (1982) calls "we-ness." Cohesiveness is a form of togetherness that keeps the group on the right path regardless of differences and individuals' agendas. In part, the responsibility for the group's cohesiveness lies with the leader. The chapter on group leadership will deal more fully with the characteristics of a good leader, or as he is more properly called, a "facilitator." Other factors also affect cohesiveness, such as; problem group members; lack of a clear understanding of the group's goal; and such trivial considerations as place and time of the group meetings. It should be noted that a group may appear to be cohesive in nature, but that the cohesiveness is in reality an evidence of the highly unlikely coincidence that the group is made up of members who are all psychologically damaged and are all "playing the game" of compliance. An effective leader will be able to diagnose this problem and either disbands the group in despair or change the physical make-up of the group.

2. Sensitivity - When the individuals of a group learn to be sensitive to the needs and feelings of others in the group, the group will succeed in moving toward healing. One of the main goals of a good Christian Growth Group is to bring the members into spiritual maturity, which requires the ability to be sensitive to other people's needs and feelings. Many people are not aware of the

difference between sympathy and empathy. Some group members will not enter into the spirit of the group if they sense that some of the group members are "feeling sorry for them" or "pitying them." For many people, the road to true spiritual maturity is much longer than for others. One group experience may not be adequate to bring about the kind of growth needed. However, even some growth is better than none at all.

3. Here and Now - The Christian Growth Group that is successful in dealing with the here and now, as opposed to the then and later, has a much greater chance of being a good group. The group needs to deal with feelings that they are experiencing now in the midst of the group. This is not the place to talk about things that happened in the distant past or things that may happen in the future. This quality of a good group also suggests that the group deals with the needs and feelings of the people that are "here" in the group and not with individuals from their past or even with individuals in their future that may cause them problems. This is not to infer that most of the problems that individuals experience in interpersonal relationships are not the result of families of dysfunction of various degrees. What it does mean is that the important issue is how those experiences are affecting one's behavior in the present.

4. Safe - A group that is safe is one in which the members feel trust in the sincerity and integrity of the other members. One of the major dynamics of a good group is "self-disclosure," which will not take place if the members do not trust one another. Members must feel that whatever is shared in the group will not be shared with anyone outside the group. This sense of confidentiality is vital in all forms of counseling, but especially in the group setting. One person in a group can destroy the group, if there is the slightest fear by the other members that some or all of the feelings and needs in the group are being shared outside the group situation. This writer has had to request on more than one occasion that a person not return to the group after it was discovered that the person had been telling her friends everything that was shared confidentially in the

group. It should be noted here, even though the matter will be taken up in greater detail in the chapter on leadership, occasionally, the leader of a new group will become aware that someone (occasionally more than one) will get into the group, simply because of their need for the security they feel. The group will most likely not be of much help to them. As soon as the present group is terminated, they will seek the security of another. They are more interested in the security they feel than in any kind of psychological healing they might obtain.

5. Empathetic- Most individuals with interpersonal or emotional problems are not looking for sympathy. Many of them have had all of the sympathy that they can stand. What is needed, and what is most healing, is understanding and empathy. When the members of a group learn how to feel with others, the group has a much better chance of moving forwards toward healing. Members need to learn the principle of "walking in the shoes of the other person," to be able to be an effective source of healing. Compassion is important, but empathy is healing. The prophet in the Old Testament expressed it best when he said, "*I came to the exiles who lived at Tel Abib near the Kebar River. And there, where they were living, I sat among them for seven days — overwhelmed.*" (Ezekiel 3:15, NIV). Sitting where others sit is another way of saying, "I have felt with them (not for them)."

SOME OF THE MORE POPULAR TYPES OF GROUPS

Although the author will note over and over in this text that regardless of the type of group, the dynamics of the group, will result in healing and growth for most of the members of the group. Researchers have shown that even in a group as structured as a Sunday school class, given the right type of leadership, spiritual and emotional growth in addition to the obvious attainment of Biblical knowledge will take place.

TASK GROUPS:

This is a group that is formed to accomplish a specific task. This could include the church committee to select the carpeting for the new sanctuary, or the committee to purchase a new church organ. Many churches have a "pulpit committee" whose task is to select a minister for consideration as the church's new pastor. The important consideration with regard to Task Groups is that each member should be selected carefully on the basis of their qualifications to focus on the specific task of the group. An individual that is totally tone deaf would not be able to contribute much in a positive way to the organ selection committee. The task group may also serve to develop Sunday School organization and curriculum, prepare individuals for church membership, develop and execute a youth camp program or special project. The concept of a Task Group is a group formed for the purpose of planning and putting into operation any task. Too often, churches leave all of the planning up to the pastor or a few members of the congregation. The difficulty with this system is that many people are not happy with the plans or decisions that the pastor or that small group of willing people make. The Task Group does not usually meet to deal with their own problems, but to achieve a goal common to all. It must be noted that, regardless of the reason a group may meet, if the group stays together for any length of time, the same dynamics will take place that occur in any other group.

COUNSELING GROUPS:

The primary function of this type of group is to meet the needs of the members of the group. There are many important advantages to the use of Counseling Groups in the church milieu. Most pastors are not physically able to meet and counsel with every individual in the church who may have some emotional or interrelational problems. The Counseling Group can take much of the burden for this need off of the pastor. The most important consideration in the use of counseling groups is the qualification of spiritual, emotional stability of the leader of such a group. Care must also be used in the selection of the persons who will participate in the group.

Severely disturbed individuals and certain borderline personalities are best left to the professional counselor on a one on one basis, because these seriously disturbed people suffer with the inability to deal with reality. Strong leaders, with the help and support of the ministerial staff can become a very strong force for good in the church, but considerable harm can come from trying to deal with severely dysfunctional people in group counseling situations. On the other hand, there are many churches and church leaders who are either afraid of groups, or are just plain opposed to anything that sounds like psychology or counseling.

FELLOWSHIP GROUPS:

This type of group is designed to meet the needs of people who are basically well-adjusted individuals in need of a more specialized type of fellowship. These groups might include: Widows groups, Singles groups, Military wives groups, new converts groups, etc. The list can be very long. It must not be thought that this type of group is strictly for socializing. People in the listed categories have needs that cannot always be met through casual social contact.

The Fellowship Group should be as well-planned and under the leadership of as good a leader as any of the therapy groups discussed in this book. Most likely, the greatest need of people in Fellowship Groups has to do with dealing with loneliness, and in some cases, low self-esteem issues. Fellowship groups do not need to always be well-planned or organized activities, but occasionally, the use of a well-planned Fellowship Group can meet the needs of many people who may simply fall through the cracks.

TRAINING GROUPS (T-GROUPS):

As the name implies, this type of group has training as its goal. T-Groups are used to train management level personnel how to more effectively deal with personnel problems in the work place. A T-Group may be formed to help teachers and staff work more effectively in a multicultural neighborhood school. Police may be trained to handle gang situations more effectively through training in a T-Group. This type of T-Group is similar to a sensitivity group in that they both endeavor to help people become more sensitive and understanding of other cultures.

The T-Group differs from a regular classroom setting, where a teacher instructs participants in effective methods of doing things. The group allows for members to share in the teaching process and deal with specific problems that they face each day. It is the opinion of many that young prospective ministers graduate from Bible College with a considerable amount of theological knowledge, but they are ill equipped to handle the relationships they will encounter in the pastorate. Interpersonal relationships can only be learned in a situation designed to promote the ability to relate to others in a healthy manner.

ENCOUNTER GROUPS:

The Encounter Group became very popular in the 60's and 70's There were many variations on this type of group. The Western Behavioral Sciences Institute in La Jolla, California was one of the leading promoters of this type of Therapy Group. Gestalt psychologists also found that the Encounter Group was an effective method of "getting in touch with feelings" This type of group requires a highly skilled counselor. People that benefit from this type of group are those who have severe to mild emotional problems that are the result of unhealthy family situations. Individuals who have been abused, physically, emotionally, sexually, or in any other way, often will bury the feelings that they experienced as a child. This process is known as sublimation. The fact that the abuse is not remembered in the conscious mind does not mean that it is no longer a problem.

Many interpersonal relationships that are dysfunctional are the result of one or more of the people involved having been raised in a dysfunctional family themselves. One of the advantages of the Encounter Group is that with the proper leadership, members can deal with their dysfunctional lifestyle in a relatively safe environment instead of the usual hostile environment of the marriage or family of origin.

In their book, Meier, Paul, etc. al. (1991) makes special mention of the Encounter Group that began in the late 1960's and 1970's. The Encounter Group emphasized utter honesty, and intimate relationships with other Group Members. These authors ask the question, "Are such groups beneficial?" They suggest that although this type of small group may help people to share more, there is a possibility of danger. Some of the individuals may not be able to cope with the utter honesty required. The writers go on to suggest that "sometimes participants verbally attack one another or apply artificial labels to other group members."

The text goes on however, to mention that one of the authors participated in such a group. All of the members were Christians and they looked forward to each of the weekly meetings. It is the opinion of this writer that in any group, whether Encounter Group, T-Group, or whatever, if the facilitator (leader) is well trained and possesses the attributes of a good leader, all of the negative aspects of the Encounter Group can be avoided. Encounter Groups or other types of groups may be either positive or negative, depending on the leadership. The author agrees with the Small Group Guidelines suggested by Meier, ET. al., in a *Spotlight* on page 328, where they suggest, along with Back (1972), that any dangers can be minimized when certain guidelines are followed:

1. Avoid labeling behavior and people. Labeling changes people's perceptions of others and themselves and may actually make genuine self-expression less likely. There are writers who advocate the eliminating of labels altogether. Instead of thinking of an individual as being a sociopath (having a sociopathic personality), it would be more conducive to healing, to describe the deviant behavior of that individual as being evident of early interactions with their parents. Parental neglect, cruelty and inconsistency provided the child with an atmosphere which is conducive to the development of antisocial behavior. Many other behavioral characteristics may be used to describe this individual,

but the label, "sociopath," is probably the most damaging in terms of progress toward healing.

2. Make verbal participation voluntary for group members. Never coerce others into talking about a topic or themselves. Coercion, or even what might seem as mild insistence to get certain people talking, may either cause them to become less willing to share, or force them to begin sharing something that is completely false, or at least, irrelevant to the person's true problems.

3. Make sure the group has a good leader who is able to take charge if things get out of control. More will be said about the leader in a separate chapter, but at this time some researchers would consider this requirement as being of prime importance when discussing the possibility of a successful group.

4. Maintain confidentiality. Free expression should be encouraged in the group, but what is discussed should not go outside the group. This requires mature members. Confidentiality must be considered as a sacred trust.

5. Avoid embarrassment and putting people on the spot. Be kind in your honesty. As with the use of coercion to get people to talk, endeavoring to get people involved in the activities of the group through the use of pressure and embarrassment, can only lead to confusion and dead ends with some individuals.

6. Only include people who are emotionally balanced. Those who have severe emotional problems require professional counseling and perhaps group counseling with other emotionally disturbed people. This has been noted before, but it may be wise to note that in case of any doubt about the stability of an individual, it would be best to refer them to a professional for testing, or at least use one of the many screening tests that are available for this purpose.

7. Keep the group spiritually based. Make regular use of Bible study and prayer. (Authors Note: One problem here is the "Bible

Thumper" who will want to solve everyone's problems with a verse of scripture. More will be presented in the chapter that deals with group members).

The Encounter Group is one of the groups that requires the careful selection (or exclusion) of potentially problematic members.

THERAPY GROUPS:

Although there is considerable healing that takes place in almost any good group, the term Therapy Group is usually used to refer to groups that are held in a hospital setting under the leadership of a psychiatrist or a clinical psychologist especially trained in therapy type groups. Participants in these types of groups are usually moderately to seriously borderline personality types. They are often confined to the hospital and under medication for their disorder. This is not to say that therapy cannot happen in a Christian group organized for the purpose of dealing with personal interrelational problems. Healing takes place at many different levels and to this extent other groups are also Therapy Groups. The Christian counselor must be familiar with the extreme psychological problems that would make an individual an unfit participant in the "normal" group setting. Many group counselors will administer a test such as the Minnesota Multiphasic Personality Inventory (MMPI) to make sure that an individual who might be considered a borderline personality does not become a member of the group. This is necessary for many reasons. Probably the most important reason is that the borderline personality individual would certainly cause a serious disruption in the dynamics of the group.

An important note about the use of personality inventories (especially those like the MMPI that give specific names to the types of personality) is to avoid, at any cost, the use of those names, or labels, in reference to the members of the group. An individual who is suffering from some level of emotional disturbance may easily be "pushed over the edge" if he is labeled a sociopath. This is especially true if that labeling comes from the authority figure or the group leader. It is safer to discuss problems of interpersonal relationships, or to suggest that an individual is having a problem relating to other people, than to suggest that the individual is a sociopath because of a high score on that part of a personality inventory.

It has been argued, by some in the past, that this type of group is reserved for the psychiatric hospital, and in some severe cases this is true. The fact is healing can take place in almost any loving, caring environment, such as a Christian Counseling Group. The great majority of people will never be in the care of a psychiatrist. Many have mild and often more than mild emotional problems resulting in strained interpersonal relationships.

MARATHON GROUPS:

Counseling Groups and Christian Growth Groups work well in the marathon mode. The main advantage of the Marathon Group is that of breaking down defenses. Because the Marathon Group meets for a long period of time in one meeting (Friday, 7-12, Saturday 8am-10pm and Sunday 8am- 4 or 5 pm), the group will begin to let down their defenses as they become weary after several hours. This has been demonstrated time and again through research. The Marathon Group, as well as some of the others, will use certain games such as: role playing, hot seat, etc., to help the group get started. This was particularly noted in the studies of the dynamics of groups in the bomb shelter in England. The longer the air raid lasted; the more open and disclosing the individuals in the group became. Some researchers in group dynamics, and many Christian critics of groups, have posited that the Marathon Group is a form of sensory deprivation which can cause serious harm to the psyche of certain individuals.

Much has been written about the brainwashing techniques used by the Vietnamese using severe sensory depravation. The Marathon Group, however, does not last so long that any serious sensory depravation would take place. The members are always free to leave the group for a period or a "time-out" or to take time to go to the bathroom. Food is also provided in the form of snacks so that the subjects are not deprived of much in the way of physical needs. It is true that the Marathon Group lasts for a considerable length of time, and that as the participants become physically tired; they tend to become more open with the group.

A doctoral project, in which this author was asked to participate, showed films of a Marathon Group that was conducted at San Diego State University... At each session of the research study, the participants were asked to view a portion of film shown out of chronological sequence. They were then asked to indicate on a form that was designed for the purpose, to mark at what hour of the marathon the film was made. The final doctoral dissertation indicated a rather high level of correlation, meaning that individuals with even a little training could predict the dynamics of the Marathon Group. However, Christian Growth Groups and many of the other Counseling Groups do not look favorably on the use of games.

CARE GROUPS:

Care groups take on many different forms. The past few years have brought on the age of the mega church. Churches with a membership of 5000 or more are becoming more common. One of the things that happened with the advent of the mega church is that pastors and leaders began to realize there was a large diversity and complexity of needs represented by this large number of people. The church needed to make provision for meeting those needs in new and innovative ways. One of the new ways adopted by these large churches was the "Cell Group Ministry." Smaller churches had for years been involved in Counseling Groups, but for a different reason.

For a number of years after the first Christian Growth Groups began to appear in churches around the country, many of the old line fundamentalist pastors denounced them as being worldly (because of the use of some psychology) or down right demonic. A few of the most outspoken preachers may have actually avoided the fall into disgrace if they had been able to be in one of those early groups.

When I first attempted to start a Christian Growth Group in San Diego, I asked a pastor friend of mine if it would be possible to organize and conduct a group in his church. His comment was, "I really don't care for all that group stuff. To me it is like turning over a rock and finding all sorts of creepy crawly things under there, things that I would rather not see."

I replied to him, "The very fact that I know that those creepy crawly things are there makes me want, with all of my heart, to get them out into the open and once and for all, smash them out of my life." The pastor was not impressed, and the subject was not approached again. It might be added that this same pastor had at that time a rather serious problem with alcohol.

The larger churches began developing cell groups patterned after the ministry of Younggi Cho in Korea. However, in order to meet the specialized need of many of the people in the large churches, pastors began developing specialized types of groups. Some of the many different types are:

GOD AND GOVERNMENT CARE GROUP:

This group meets periodically to discuss the Christian's role in politics from a biblical perspective. Although this would not normally be considered a Counseling Group, there are many times when real therapy will take place as a result of the interchange of ideas. Unfortunately, the more militant individual is most attracted to this type of group as a forum for his or her own personal agenda. This type of group must have a strong and well-trained leader to keep certain group members from taking over and dominating every group meeting. It is this type of group that might meet to formulate plans to oppose abortion. There is much to be said about a group of concerned Christians meeting together to discuss and plan action against the forces who advocate abortion as opposed to a disorganized group (or mob) breaking laws and causing more harm than good to the right to life movement.

Hispanic CARE Groups:

Especially in certain large metropolitan areas, Hispanics often develop unique kinds of emotional, economic, and health problems that can be helped through the CARE group ministry. The church with even a small Hispanic population can provide very valuable assistance to this ethnic culture through the use of Hispanic Care Groups. This is also true of other ethnic groups. Leadership of this type of group requires that the leader be at least aware of the principles taught in cross-cultural counseling courses.

CARE Groups for the Hearing Impaired:

Because of the needs of the hearing impaired, for meaningful relationships and fellowship, the CARE group ministry is best suited to help meet those needs. People with like disabilities can relate to other members of this type of group with much more empathy than a person who is not hearing impaired. It would seem that a hearing impaired individual would make the best leader for such a group.

Singles' CARE Groups:

Here again is a special group of people with special needs. Many singles do not feel uneasy about their singleness. There are many, however, who experience serious emotional problems as singles. The fact is that some people look at singles and wonder why they never married. There are some people who would even suggest that there may be a problem of homosexuality. The single person is well-aware of the thoughts and suspicions of others and as a result experience feelings of guilt or shame. One of the most prevailing problems experienced by singles is that of low self-esteem. This type of group is an excellent medium in which these people may learn to overcome the guilt and shame and also develop better self-esteem.

Young Marrieds' CARE Groups:

Young people are seldom prepared for the special kinds of

relational problems that occur in marriage. Premarital counseling is a great help in preparing young people for the "great step," but all too often the two young people in love, seldom take seriously the admonitions of the pastor before marriage. The increase in marital dissolution in modem society in America is an indication that young people are not properly prepared for a life commitment.

This increasing incidence of spousal and child abuse is also an indicator that something is wrong with the preparation that young people are receiving before marriage. One way to help young marrieds adjust to the demands of a completely new style of life found in marriage is the Young Marrieds' Group. In these groups, young married people can learn to confide their fears, anxieties, and other concerns about married life, before they find themselves out of control and guilty of some abusive or otherwise destructive behavior.

The Young Marrieds' CARE Group is not to be thought of as merely a social gathering, although this group of people really does need the social contacts that can come from such a group. Every church should have, in addition to a Young Marrieds' CARE Group, a Young Marrieds' Fellowship and if possible a Sunday school class for that part of the congregation.

Youth CARE Groups:

With all of the pressures on young people in modem society, there is a great need to minister to them in the small group situation. Large youth rallies are fine and have a place in the ministry of the church, but individual needs are seldom met or even addressed at such rallies. The teenager probably represents the greatest challenge to a Christian community. Anyone who has taken the time to study the literature about the physical, emotional, moral and spiritual problems experienced by the teenager knows that this is a stage of great upheaval. It is not enough to bash the teen over the head with the scriptures that forbid certain behavior. Teens are already experiencing a traumatic struggle with the authority of their parents and other adults in their lives. They are struggling with feelings that are very new and extremely strong. They experience physical urges that are perhaps the strongest feelings a human can experience.

A strong, patient, and understanding leader can help teens share their common problems in an atmosphere that is neither condemning nor unfeeling. A good leader will not only have his or her own personal journey through adolescence to draw upon, but they will hopefully be trained as a leader on the subject of human development. (See, Human Development: A Christian Perspective, also by this author.)

Children's CARE Groups:

These groups may take on many forms. There may be groups for children from abusive homes, groups for children with special physical limitations, etc. The prospects are as unlimited as the imagination.

Seniors' CARE Groups:

Seniors often feel left out of the mainstream of the church's activities. Most churches, especially the larger ones, are youth oriented, and seniors simply must sit around on the fringes and observe. One of the greatest needs for Christian CARE is with the seniors who are left behind through the death (or divorce) of a mate. In recent years a new kind of abuse has come to the attention of the authorities - elder abuse. As the American society becomes more upwardly mobile economically, there seems to be less interest in caring for the "old folks." In years past, young people often took care of their aging parents in their own home. Everyone gained. The children gained from the love and wisdom of the grandparents, and the grandparents were not subjected to the insult and injury of being placed in an uncaring rest home. Granted, it was not all perfect, but the tendency is moving toward the mistreatment and abandonment of elders. This is, of course, against the teachings of the Word of God.

" Do not sharply rebuke an older man, but rather appeal to him as *a father, to the younger men as brothers, the older women as mothers, and the younger women as sisters, in all purity."* (1 Timothy 5:1-2).

"Do not receive an accusation against an elder except on the basis of two or three witnesses." (I Timothy 5:19).

"Therefore, I exhort the elders among you, as your fellow elder and witness of the sufferings of Christ, and a partaker also of the glory that is to be revealed," (I Peter 5:1).

"You younger men, likewise, be subject to your elders; and all of you, clothe yourselves with humility toward one another, for GOD IS OPPOSED TO THE PROUD, BUT GIVES GRACE TO THE HUMBLE." (I Peter 5:5).

RECOVERY GROUPS OF ALL TYPES:

These may include: Recovering Alcoholics, Recovering Drug Addicts, Recovering Homosexuals, Recovering Children of Alcoholic or Abusive Parents, Recovering Victims of Abuse (Sexual, Physical, etc.), Recovering Overeaters, Recovering Anorexics, and on and on the list may go. The Word of God commissions the Christian to be active in the ministry of restoration.

"Brethren, even if anyone is caught in any trespass, you who are spiritual, restore such a one in a spirit of gentleness; each one looking to yourself, so that you too will not be tempted". (Galatians 6:1).

"Now all these things are from God, who reconciled us to Himself through Christ and gave us the ministry of reconciliation, namely, that God was in Christ reconciling the world to Himself, not counting their trespasses against them, and He has committed to us the word of reconciliation." (II Corinthians 5:18-19).

The Lord has settled our relations with Himself, and now he calls on us to settle our relationship with one another. This is precisely what groups purport to do.

The name of the group isn't as important as the need that it addresses. One of the needs of every church is to ascertain what the needs of the congregation are and develop ministries to meet those needs.

Evangelism:

One of the benefits of the group ministries that really surprised many pastors is that when a church begins offering CARE group ministries, the word will soon get around the community and before long people who may never come into the church for any other reason will come to one of the groups. It is not unreasonable to believe that once these unchurched people discover the healing power of the Christian environment, they will almost certainly become involved in the other activities such as the worship services.

When a church develops a counseling center as a part of the church ministry, they almost always begin to see new people coming to the church. As mentioned earlier, groups have been seen by many church leaders as a means of revitalizing churches that have begun to lose appeal for the world. A truly hurting world needs more than theology and beautiful hymns on Sunday to heal the hurts. There is a need for a community in which they may find understanding and also learn how to deal more effectively with their problems.

Some years ago while I was a student in Bible College; I recall an incident that made me realize how truly ill-equipped most people are to deal with the real problems of man. A young classmate of mine was having some serious problems with his sexual orientation. He went to the Dean of Men, who was a veteran of the foreign mission field having spent many years in India. The advice that the Dean gave this young man was not only strange, but futile. The young student was told to read the Book of Ephesians everyday and to pray for the Lord to deliver him.

I believe in the power of prayer and in the hope that can be gained from reading the Holy Scriptures, but in this case, what this young man needed was understanding and caring counsel to see him through this crisis.

SENSORY AWARENESS GROUPS

This type of group is relatively new. The goal of the technique is to help members become more aware of sensory experiences as well as to discover the effects of sensory deprivation. (The Colossus Ride at Magic Mountain theme park in California is an example of sensory awareness).

CHRISTIAN GROWTH GROUPS:

The Christian Growth Group does not appear on the chart of groups because this type of group activity did not begin until the middle seventies and was primarily a function of the church. A number of Christian group styles began developing in the early 1970's. One such group was the *Yokefellow's* founded by Cecil Osborn in Burlingame, California. This group technique involved the use of the Minnesota Multiphasic Personality Inventory (MMPI) and the DAP (Draw A Person,) as a guide to help group members uncover areas of their personality that needed healing or simply change. The groups met for about thirteen weeks, and every other week each member of the group received an evaluation slip to share with the group. Much of Chapter 6 will deal with different techniques that can be used in the Christian Growth Group. The Yokefellow's organization developed many other tests that could be used in a similar fashion such as a Married Couples Test, A Youth Inventory, etc.

Bruce Larson and other Christian leaders developed their own "Adventures in Christian Living" groups. Keith Miller wrote a book and produced an audio tape that was used to guide group members through various exercises (adventures) in Christian growth. There will be more on this in Chapter 6.

The Christian Growth Groups, as they have come to be known at Logos Christian Center in San Diego, California, under the leadership of Dr. Joseph J. Bohac, were somewhat like the Encounter Groups mentioned earlier, except that these groups were not as confrontive, but were tempered with Christian love and compassion. The Christian Growth Group would come under the classification of a Counseling Group. The goal of the counseling group and the Christian Growth Group is basically the same: healing that will facilitate spiritual growth. The chart in Figure 1 illustrates the stages in Group Dynamics (see pages 60-63).

"The secret of many a man's success in the world resides in his insight into the moods of men and his tact in dealing with them."
J. G. Holland

CHAPTER 2:

GROUP DYNAMICS

Early famous pioneers in the field of sociology saw society as being largely static, that is society tended to stay basically the same over the years. It was much later that Lester Ward published his work, *Dynamic Sociology* (1893). Sociologists began to think of society as being dynamic or in a constant state of change. Applied to the field of group counseling, the term dynamics suggests that a group will naturally follow a pattern of change. It was not until recent times that investigators began to realize that organized groups not only change, but they change in a predictable pattern. This hypothesis was tested a number of times with the same results. One such investigation was conducted at Western Behavioral Science Institute in La Jolla, California, in conjunction with United States International University.

A Marathon Group was held on Friday evening, all day Saturday, and on Sunday until noon for a total of 24 hours. The entire 24 hours was filmed. Several groups of doctoral students were asked to view different sections of the film and indicate, on a prepared form, the hour (or stage) that the film depicted. The results of the survey were a part of a doctoral dissertation and were subjected to statistical analysis. It was concluded that the progress of a typical Marathon Group could be accurately predicted because the dynamics (changes) were similar to all groups.

According to Bonner (1959), "Behavior itself, whether individual or collective, is dynamic if changes or adjustments in one 'part' are followed by changes or adjustments in all the others." He goes on to say that, a dynamic group then, is not a collection of interdependent individuals, merely, but a group of persons who are psychologically aware of their inter-individual relationships and who are moving toward a goal that they have agreed upon collectively.

The dynamics of a group is partly attributable to the process that Ward called group wisdom. The wisdom of the group has reference to the group solution of a problem or problems (Bonner, 1959). This same group wisdom that works in social groups is what seems to take place in the Counseling Group.

Figure 1 shows some of the stages in Group Dynamics. The chart adapted from Dibbert and Wichern (1985) shows four stages and three different concerns in Group Dynamics. The stages are 1) Orientation (Trust building and disclosure). It is in this stage that the first preliminary disclosures form by members sharing a brief history of their lives. This can be a very important time of disclosure because members will risk only a little of their real self in order to "feel out" the group. The effectiveness of later disclosures will depend to a great extent on how well they are accepted.

The chart in Figure 1 will demonstrate the stages of development of the group. It is important to note that unless the group is highly structured and dominated by a very autocratic leader, the stages, as they are listed, will most certainly follow in a sequential invariant order. That is, the stages will follow one another in order, and in most cases at about the same interval of time.

The first stage is the time when the boundaries of the group are set. Such seemingly unimportant matters as setting times for the meetings, making the reading assignments, and setting the expected standard for the group can provide the leader with important insights. An individual member who seems to resist the setting of assignments or the emphasizing of the importance of punctuality and regular attendance may prove to be dealing with some severe issue of resentment toward authority figures. Knowledge of these attitudes can help the leader later in the growth of the group. Dibbert and Wichern (1985) found that the individual member concerns included questions that primarily involve their own acceptance in the group, the trustworthiness of the group, what can be expected out of this activity, and what will be expected of me as to participation.

The leader's main concerns have to do with setting a good tone for the group. However, more than that the leader will be looking for possible problem members of the group. If one member seems to want to "preach" or simply has many opinions during this stage, the leader will need to deal with that situation before much growth will take place. The leader at this first stage of the Group Dynamics will also wish to watch closely for the individual in the group who may best serve as a co-facilitator (if one has not already been assigned).

FIGURE 1

STAGES IN GROUP GROWTH AND CHANGE

Stage	Small Group Concerns	Member Concerns	Leader Concerns
Stage One Orientation (Trust Building and Disclosure)	Members begin to disclose through brief history. Where should our meeting take us? What should individuals expect from meetings? How long do we meet? How many times? Can people be late? What clothes are acceptable, etc.? Who is our leader? Why is he/she the leader? How committed should members be?	What do I want out of these meetings? What are growth groups about? Will I be accepted? What will I do or participate in? Are these people trustworthy? Am I going to attend this group? What are we going to do?	Needs to give personal history to begin disclosure. Needs to think through what to say to set the level of disclosure. Watches for members who want to "lecture" or "preach"; encourages people to not give advice but listen. At the end of the first meeting, discusses need for commitment and trust by talking about confidentiality.

Stage	Small Group Concerns	Member Concerns	Leader Concerns
Stage Two Transition Awareness Unfreezing	Members begin to express needs and goals for the meeting. Will we have conflict over our goals? Who is going to get this group moving? When can we give advice? Why should we "stay on track?"	Should I initiate? What don't I like? Am I willing to say so? What do the members want of me? Can I risk conflict? Do I cause conflict? What is listening? Why not "fix" people? Does anyone have answers? Is the leader really leading?	Needs to observe his/her own verbal and body language for agreement to model congruence. Needs to risk "feeling" messages to continue self-disclosure. Observes conflict among members. Discourages "advice giving" and using experts to inhibit self-disclosure. Resists interrupting behavior and creating dependency by "teaching." Determines who the "junior leader" is and how intense that person's needs are.

Stage	Small Group Concerns	Member Concerns	Leader Concerns
Stage Three Action Change	Members begin to recognize individual responsibility. Several members are able to create a sufficient amount of beneficial anxiety enabling the others to begin unfreezing. A general attitude of closeness and commitment emerges. Members anticipate the next meeting and positively reward each other.	Why should I change? Who am I? What do I want to get done? What is process? How do I communicate accurately, effectively? Why do people remind me of parents, friends, teachers, etc.? Why do I ask so much out of myself, others? Why do I feel pain when I face my problems? Why haven't I had relationships with friends or family like we have in the group?	There is less activity and more listening by the leader. Most comments are brief and are positive reinforcements. Be ready for the desire of the group to have a "party". Recommend another time and place. Do not smooth over conflict. Encourage healthy resolution. Attempt to use parable or process remarks to confront member's problem behaviors.

Stage	Small Group Concerns	Member Concerns	Leader Concerns
Stage Four Termination And Refreezing	Members begin to anticipate the ending. How will this group continue to function? Should this be an ongoing function? Members need to evaluate whether initial goals were met and what additional goals have been reached. Members should understand the generalization of the group behavior to other areas of their life. Members should talk about saying "goodbye."	Can I do this elsewhere? Will I keep growing? What can I take with me? Will I continue to care? Will I tell these people? What deep pains does this experience (e.g. death, leaving) arouse?	Remind the group two meetings in advance of the ending. Be prepared to reinforce something of each member's participation. Be prepared to commit or refuse member's request for additional meetings. Anticipate member's desire for life goals: when appropriate, make recommendations. Enjoy the process of change!

Stage two is one of transition. It is during this stage that the members begin to "unfreeze" and become more aware of the real needs and goals of the other members. It is at this stage that the struggle between acceptance and non-acceptance emerges. In the beginning, group members may wish to give advice each time a member expresses a need or a problem. It is here that the leader must carefully point out that the feelings being shared are real and that the sharer may have had many people give advice in the past. What the member is looking for most at this time is acceptance. The question is, "This is how I feel, can you understand and accept me with those feelings?"

It is at this stage that the members of the group begin to enter into what Lewin (1948) refers to as the "Journey into Life Space." Lewin saw the life space of the individual as a "relatively closed system which attempts to maintain equilibrium under the impact of field forces, negative and positive valences." Bates and Johnson add:

> The various life spheres (professional, family, friendships with definite persons, etc.) as well as different needs become more and more differentiated as a person expands his life space and extends physical regions and systems within his life space (Bates and Johnson, 1992). See the further discussion of life space in Chapter 4 of this text under "Non-verbal body language."

This is also the stage when members will begin weighing their participation in the group. They will wonder if what they have to share or disclose will be proper at that time. It is here also that the members will learn the skill of listening. There will also be some evaluating of the leader during this stage. Is he really leading the group? Or is the group leading him? Is the leader expected to have all the answers, or is he like the rest of the members — a fellow seeker?

It is also at this stage that the group will begin to function more in the capacity of a reflector of the feelings of the other members. As the members learn to listen with empathy, they will become more like mirrors to help the other members see themselves as others see them. In existential terms, each group member begins to "sign his or her signature to their statement of essence. It is through this stage that the members will begin to develop what Martin Buber called the "I-Thou" type of relationship with others. It is at this stage that some of the factors that determine the success or failure of the group begin to appear. Bonner (1959) speaks of the "relation of the part to the whole, or of the individual to the group" using the general science of spatial relations. The concept of valence represents the attraction or repulsion value of an object for an individual or a group. It describes disruptive forces in group relationships, or cooperation and conflict. A positive valance designates membership-character, group belongingness, a vector directed toward the same region. A negative valance designates isolation, leaving the field (or group), a vector directed away from the same region (Bonier, 1959, p. 44).

In the chapter dealing with evaluation of a group process, there will be a discussion of how this factor may be used as a measure of group effectiveness.

Stage three is called the action stage. This is a time of change. Because of the interrelationship with the other members as mirrors, the members begin to recognize individual responsibility. There begins to emerge a general feeling of camaraderie and closeness among the members. There is a growing anticipation of the next meeting. The interaction between members is one of support and positive reward. The members begin thinking in terms of "I really can change." "I can see myself more in the light of how others see me, and it isn't so bad." "Why isn't it possible to have relationships like this in everyday life?" The leader becomes less active and more of a listener. He can trust the group to function by themselves. He does not feel as anxious when conflict arises, because he knows that the group is able to handle it. The leader becomes more of a resource person at this stage.

The final stage was called termination and refreezing by Dibbert and Wichern (1985). This is the stage at which members begin to anticipate the ending of the group. They evaluate the goals that were met and the ones that were not met. There is a real feeling of oneness among the members. It is as if they all belonged to a special society of friends —friends that knew more about them than perhaps anyone else in their personal relationships. The members begin to think of how the lessons that were learned in the group will apply to their everyday relationships. "Will I have to go back to being a private person for fear that I will be rejected?" "Will it be possible for me to care for others outside the group as I have for the members of the group?" "Will I be able to share what has happened to me with my closest friends and family?" These and other questions will be foremost in the minds of the members as the group begins to wind down.

It is at this time that the leader must take the initiative in preparing the members for the end of the group. Some of the members may need to be referred to private counseling, but all of them need to feel that they are available to each other in times of need. What has happened in the group should not be an end in and of itself. The group experience can open new relationships that can last many years. What has been learned in the group can be training for each member to become a better minister or lay leader in the church.

There is a sense in which almost any type of group will have a goal to develop awareness and skill building. The Christian Growth Group, although dealing primarily with the present and future, will frequently deal with the past as it may have relevance to what is happening in the present. The major difference between the Christian Growth Group and the Therapy Group is that the Christian Growth Group tends not to dwell in the past (as might happen in a strictly Freudian therapy group). In addition, the Christian Growth Group would emphasize the importance of "... Brethren, I do not regard myself as having laid hold of it yet; but one thing I do: forgetting what lies behind and reaching forward to what lies ahead, I press on toward the goal for the prize of the upward call of God in Christ Jesus..." (Philippians 3:13-14, NKJ), this is a more sure goal of the group.

Another schematic that represents the different dynamics of Growth Groups is shown in figure 2. It was taken from one presented in the Annual Handbook for Group Facilitators, University Associates. Although the figure indicates that each type of group has some distinct differences, the Christian Growth Group will in most cases, include all of the elements to some degree or another.

FIGURE 2— THE JOHARI WINDOW

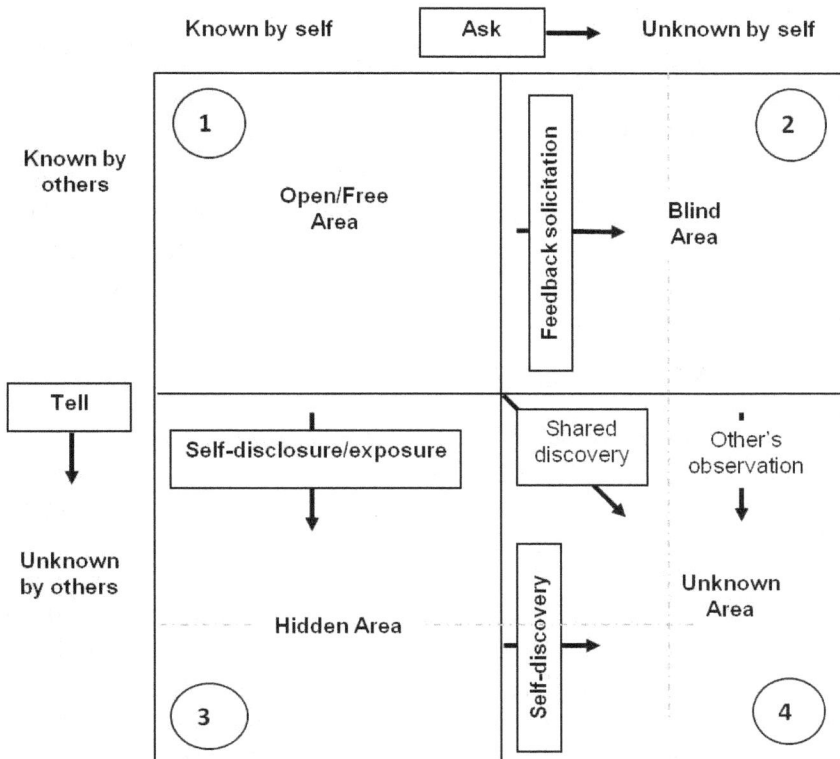

Diagram recreated by Kathy Smith 2012

In some of the Christian Growth Groups using one of the personality inventories, it is almost impossible to totally ignore the past as it related to the present and the future. It is certainly a goal of the Christian Growth Group to facilitate healing to provide comfort and to increase coping, etc. that are indicated as the goals and therapy of other groups. In other words, the Growth Group is intended to accomplish most of the functions of other groups but in the Christian context.

It is the primary function of a Christian Growth Group to help the members receive healing for those areas in their lives that are preventing them from becoming Christ-like. Surely the goal of every activity of the church is to lead people to Jesus and then to assist them in their journey to wholeness to become more like Christ. This is what James meant when he recorded. *"Therefore, confess your sins to one another, and pray for one another so that you may be healed."* (James 5:16).

It is the "one for another" aspect of Christianity that sets it apart from the other religions and philosophies of the world. As a member of the Body of Christ, each member has a responsibility to care for the other members. The health of each member depends on the health of the whole.

ROLE AND FACADE

Sociology and psychology have contributed to the study of human behavior and the concept of roles as a natural part of life. Everyone plays out several roles in everyday life. A man is at times in the role of a father, husband, manager of a department at work, or a lover to a mistress, etc. Some people have more roles than others to play out during each day. Roles are considered as special positions in groups along with early expectations of certain behaviors. Roles are usually quite explicit and well-defined. Roles may be less specific than the examples given above. In a college classroom one might find such roles as teacher's pet, the reluctant student, the persistent critical student, and so forth. These less specific roles are usually learned roles that may or may not have any significant consequences in everyday life, although they may have some affect on the grade that the student receives (Schneider, 1988).

All roles are learned. The husband for the most part learned how to behave as a husband from his relationship with his father. It is believed that this is why wife abusers had fathers who were wife abusers. The father learns the role of father from his father, etc. Role confusions usually are the result of weak or negative parental examples. The concept that the homosexual male may be the product of a weak father image and a strong domineering mother image has long been recognized by workers in the field of marriage and family relations.

One of the problems with roles is role conflict. Interrole conflict occurs when a person finds that two roles he or she plays have conflicting demands. Many people experience such role conflicts in trying to be a good spouse and parent on the one hand and a good company employee on the other (Schneider, 1988). This is particularly true of a woman who desires to be the best mother possible, but also finds that her career interferes with the desired role because she always wants to climb the career ladder to the top. College professors may experience conflict between the demands of the University for them to do significant research and at the same time devote substantial time to their students. This is called interrole conflict (Schnieder, 1988).

There are many ways in which people deal with role conflict. One is to perform different aspects of the same role at different times and places. Thus, the mother may spend super quality time with her infant on the weekends, and also spend quality time on the job during the week.

Along with role conflict comes the possibility of role confusion. The best example of role confusion comes from research in the field of adolescent psychology. During puberty, the emerging adolescent usually struggles with many questions regarding what is expected of him or her. One moment they may be told to grow up and learn to take more responsibility for their actions, but at the next moment they are told that they are too young to date or drive the car. The real problem with role confusion is that many people learn to play a role that is in conflict with their true feelings. There are times when everyone must wear the facade (false face) and act in a way that they believe they are expected to act. The young man in pursuit of a young lady's hand in marriage may act in certain ways that camouflage his true character, because he believes that the young lady would have no part of him if she knew what he was really like.

While at the PTA meeting, the father may play the part of the loving father who spends many hours helping his children with their homework, when in fact he seldom spends any time with them at all. He knows that a good father is expected to behave is such a way, and rather than have people think less of him, he dons the mask of the character of the good father and plays the role.

The problem with masks and role conflicts is that they extract a real toll in terms of emotional stability. It is very stressful to always be playing the part of someone else. The possibility of letting down the mask is ever present, risking being exposed for what one truly is. Some people have a need to play many roles as a result of faulty parenting or emotionally devastating experiences in their early childhood. With these people it is much like being in a swimming pool and trying to hold underwater several beach balls at the same time. With great effort the individual may succeed in holding down the ball for a considerable amount of time, but sooner or later the task becomes so difficult that the beach balls begin to surface. In a maddening effort to gain control, the person may well have what can only be called an emotional explosion. Many interpersonal relationships end with this type of explosion.

Jesus referred to this phenomenon when he said,

> *"Woe to you, scribes and Pharisees, hypocrites! For you are like whitewashed tombs which on the outside appear beautiful, but inside they are full of dead men's bones and all uncleanness. So you, too,*

outwardly appear righteous to men, but inwardly you are full of hypocrisy and lawlessness." (Matthew 23:27-28).

An interesting example of this concept happened in a Christian Growth Group that I was conducting at Logos Christian Center in San Diego. Herb and his wife, both solid members of the local Lutheran Church, often attended the Christian Fellowship at Logos. Logos was Charismatic in its form of worship and believed in and practiced the gifts of the Holy Spirit including prayer for the sick. The Lutheran Church was not in any way accepting of the doctrinal or theological stance of Logos.

At one of the group meetings, the members had all received their evaluation slip from the MMPI. The meeting started with different members sharing there slips with the rest of the group. Herb read his slip that indicated that he had some problems with what other people thought of him. He adamantly suggested that this slip had really misinterpreted him, even though he understood that the test only reflected on the answers that he had given on that test. He insisted that he was not in the least concerned about what others thought about him. They could accept him as he was or not. It really didn't matter to him. His wife smiled but did not say a word. After some discussion, the group went on to other things.

At one time toward the end of the session, someone asked about dreams. They had had a dream and wondered what it meant. Some discussion followed. Herb interjected that he had had a dream the previous night. He related his dream. "I was in church at Logos. They were laying on hands and praying for people at the front of the church, and my wife and I were there praying also. As I was praying for the healing of one individual and I happened to look toward the entrance to the chapel. There at the entrance were several of the board members of my home church. I became very concerned that they would see me and my wife there laying hands on and praying for this individual's healing." When he finished telling his dream, the rest of the group could not hold back their amusement. He wondered what had amused them. Suddenly he realized that the MMPI evaluation had not been completely wrong. He was very much concerned about what certain people thought about him.

Group counseling may be the best place for individuals to learn to let down the masks that they have learned to wear. There are exceptions to the rule, but most people would find that they would be accepted just as well without the facade. It is a wonderful relief to discover that it is possible to "just be yourself" without the emotional weight of trying to be several other people because of the fear of rejection.

GROUP DYNAMICS AND PERSONALITY DYNAMICS

The behavior of a group cannot be judged solely on the basis of the personality variables of its members. Other factors influence the behavior of the group.

Modern social psychologists agree that personality is effectively molded by the group in which the child is socialized. Modern dynamists are of one mind in believing that the attitudes and behaviors of persons are modified by their membership in referenced groups (Bonner, 1959). Bonner continues by suggesting that all groups are to some extent affected by the personality of their members, making Group Dynamics and personality dynamics inseparable.

The dynamic of a group is affected by many factors: leadership style, personality dynamics of the leaders, personality of individuals in the group, etc. Bonner mentions several additional factors that also determine the direction of the group. These factors are summarized in the following:

The Pressure Towards Conformity - For the most part, the effect of the group upon the person is a pressure toward conformity. This is also thought of as a pressure toward uniformity. This pressure is the result of the individual personality and beliefs of each of the members. The pressure toward conformity is the result in turn of the directive force of group norms and standards. The degree of conformity or uniformity that results from a group norm depends on the cohesiveness of the group. The more cohesive the group, the more it tends to influence its members to conform to its standards. The less cohesive the group, the more it induces deviant behavior. This point can most dramatically be illustrated through the observance of groups such as Alcoholics Anonymous and other groups for addictive behavior.

Group pressure and attitudinal change - Attitudes seldom change in response to persuasion, propaganda, appeals to good will, and similar influences. Lewin's (1939) experiment in changing food habits, and other studies have shown that attitudes change most readily when an entire group makes its own decisions regarding important problems. Studies show that as the pressure for conformity increases, the magnitude of change in opinion and attitudes also changes. This has been supported by studies by Festinger and Thibaut (1951) using low, medium, and high pressure and found that there was a significant correlation between the level of pressure and the level of conformity. This fact shows the potential power of the small group in changing attitudes and behavior.

It should be noted here that this dynamic in groups can be either good or bad. The brainwashing techniques used by the communists in Asian countries were a good example of this fact. The attitudes and behaviors of prisoners were influenced negatively by the pressure of the attitude adjustment groups conducted by the prison camp officials.

Group pressure and performance - A study conducted by Brehm and Festinger on the influence of pressure on performance in a group showed that the pressure to conform is effective in the situation described, and it furthermore suggests that the degree of the pressure can be as important as the ability of the person. As the pressure increases often the ability increases.

PERSONALITY VARIABLES IN GROUP BEHAVIOR

The Freudian View - Bonner continues to note that although some people would have trouble with the lack of empirical and experimental data in his theory of group development. It is not difficult to find a more individualistic explanation than that of Freud. Freud believed that group belongingness is based on the repression of libidinal and aggressive instincts or impulses, the repressions that are normally initiated by family life in a child's early life and transferred later to the particular group in which the adult finds himself. According to Bonner, dependence on the family is the prototype of all social groups and group processes. Although this theory seems to have some real merit, it is of course untestable.

Self-Actualization - It has been fairly well-established that groups satisfy the desire for self-actualization. Persons wish to be in groups because they afford them the opportunities to gain recognition and acceptance. Self-actualization is a way of realizing individual goals objectively, in the presence of others. This is particularly true of those groups that are organized as Task Groups, or problem solving groups.

The self-actualizing of an individual in a group depends on his or her capacity to relate to others. These individuals are not helplessly dependent upon the group. They possess a kind of autonomy and independence. Self-actualizing behavior is also characterized by a high degree of spontaneity.

In the next chapter, some of the techniques will be presented that can be used to deal with certain interpersonal relationship problems, the techniques of role playing and role reversal These are two very effective ways of dealing with role conflict and role confusion.

"To rejoice in another's prosperity, is to give content to your own lot: to mitigate another's grief, is to alleviate or dispel your own." Thomas Edwards

CHAPTER 3:

THE THERAPIST OR GROUP LEADER

In Chapter 5 of Yalom's book, *The Theory and Practice of Group Psychotherapy...* (1975), the author lists several functions of a leader, whether a therapist or simply a Christian Group leader. Group leaders are often referred to as facilitators because their main function is to see that the group accomplishes its goals.

It does not seem prudent to include an extensive discussion of the characteristics of different types of leadership style. The individual who expects to minister in healing groups, however, should spend some time reading and studying the excellent material that is available on this topic.

For the purposes of this text, a summary of the major leadership styles is presented.

Although it is not considered by many as good psychology to "type or label" people in any way, it is generally agreed that leadership styles fall into one of four categories:

Authoritarian Leadership is that style of leadership that is characterized by power and domination. Another term to describe this style of leadership would be dictatorial. The authoritarian leader is in control and "calls the shots" in almost any situation. In the group situation, this style of leadership spells certain disaster from the onset. This leader will not permit people to open-up in any kind of self-disclosure. Neither would the authoritarian permit any one else to assume the leadership role, even for a moment. These leaders are directors and controllers who will make the group move in a direction that they themselves feel would be best. One of the characteristics of the authoritarian leader is his or her frequent interruption of the member of the group who is speaking. The leader makes a habit of completing the statements before the group member is finished.

Democratic Leadership is not interested in being in control or in possession of power over others. He is interested in stimulating members of a group to work together as equals in the pursuit of a common, collective goal. He is interested in facilitating effective role behavior in others (Bonner, 1959). He is willing to serve as a resource person, but is primarily interested in the members of the group solving their own problems through interaction with one another. Bonner suggests that the characteristics of a democratic leader may be summed up best as a man with confidence in respect for human beings. The same traits that make the democratic leader the best type of facilitator for groups, also makes him or her, the best example for the group members as a role model. The personality type is considered as being "positive and healthy which will generate and sustain a democratic group atmosphere" (Bonner, 1959).

Laissez Faire Leadership is as the French implies: do nothing to disturb the status quo. This leader does little of nothing to move the group toward healing. Bonner suggests the laissez faire leader is usually a good listener and may help the group move toward cohesiveness in group thinking. The same criticism that was at one time leveled at the "non-directive" method of counseling is often leveled at the laissez faire type of leadership. It should be noted that there is a difference between a non-caring attitude and the method employed by the non-directive technique.

The laissez faire individuals are often noted for their non-evaluative attitude toward others. The true "do-nothing" type of leadership would be of little help in Group Dynamics, but the better qualities mentioned here are of great value in the group situation.

Bureaucratic leadership is the one form of leadership that is not often listed with the other three, yet so much of the leadership in modem industry, business, religion, and the armed forces are structured on the bureaucratic leadership style (Bonier, 1959).

Leaders in these organizations are expected to follow the established policies of the organization they represent. A good leader of this type is successful if he or she follows company policy to the letter. There is little room for creativity or innovation. They play by the book and insist that everyone in their charge do the same. This type of leadership implies a chain of command. Subordinates are not expected to take on any authority that has not been explicitly given to them.

In the group situation, such a leader would have a preconceived idea as to whom the leader must answer (i.e. the pastor of the church). They may not behave like the authoritarian leader in that they would not use power and authority to control the group. They would rather use coercion, persuasion, shame, and other manipulative measures to move a group in a particular direction.

Leadership Styles

Another way of looking at leadership styles is taken from the Rogerian concept of non-directive versus directive style of therapy. Carl Rogers, (1951) developed the concept of non-directive or client-centered therapy, in which the client talks about his current problems, and the therapist serves as a reflector and clarifies the client's expressed or implied emotions. The client is allowed to work out the solution to his or her own problems and is made to realize that he or she can do the same in the everyday world outside of the counseling room.

The non-directive leader is one who would help the group become reflective toward each other producing the same effect. A directive style of therapy or leadership style involves the leader deciding what course the group needs to take and then either by direct teaching or by subtle modeling, leads the group in the prescribed direction. The directive style of counseling and group leadership is steadily being replaced by the non-directive style. There seems to be little doubt that the goal of counseling whether group or individual is to help the client (group member) become responsible for his or her own recovery. It should be noted however, that the non-directive style is basically effective with people who are what would be considered "normal." Individuals with serious emotional problems would have more trouble functioning in a non-directive atmosphere.

1. The leader as a dynamo (or conductor): often the leader will be greatly influenced by the energy field of a group in action. The dynamics of groups is so amazing that an outside observer can see the group develop and change in almost predictable patterns. The more the leader is aware of these dynamics, the more effective the group will be. The casual untrained observer may have problems recognizing the group's dynamics. A trained facilitator will be aware of where the group is dynamics-wise and will also know what to expect next. The facilitator may function like a symphony conductor. He or she helps the group follow the score but allows for variations of the theme.

2. The leader is actually a creator in that he is responsible for creating and convening the group. The success of a group depends upon the methods used by the leader in convening the group and in the way the first meeting or two are conducted. If the leader takes the wrong kind of lead, i.e. becomes too directive, he may lead the group into a completely unnatural group process that will result in disappointing end results. Once the group has been led astray preventing the natural group dynamics to function, it is almost impossible to get them back on track. In this respect, the leader is also responsible for orchestrating and maintaining an atmosphere conducive to good healthy interaction.

3. The leader is a gatekeeper in that he functions to prevent member attrition. There will be members of almost any group who will become discouraged or experience such anxiety that they will want to drop out of the group. It is the responsibility of the group leader to stay focused on the group members in such a way that whoever wishes to drop out, will be encouraged before they have a chance to actually leave the group. There are times when other members of the group will be aware of this problem and will either alert the leader or actually function as the encourager. The

"official" group leader must not feel threatened by other group members taking the lead in a group session. It is healthy to see other members of the group taking the leadership role from time to time. It is important for the facilitator to prevent any one person from totally usurping complete control of the group. This will be discussed further in the section on "problem group members."

4.   The leader serves as the common denominator in the group and may become the target, if problems arise in a group of emotionally charged individuals. This happens in individual counseling and is called transference, that is when the member of the group transfers his of her feeling to the group leader. Transference is a normal and healthy process, and a good leader will take advantage of this occurrence and use it as a vehicle of learning. As much as is possible the leader must be in touch with not only his feelings, but also the feelings of the others in the group. Again, the facilitator must be willing to allow other members of the group to feel free to bring to the leader's attention something that is taking place in the group that the leader may have missed.

5.   The leader is the protector of the group's cohesiveness, as well as protecting individual members from the wrong kind of interaction (labeling or excessive hostility). Cohesiveness has to do with togetherness. This togetherness can be destroyed if members of the group feel threatened by or are aggressively antagonistic toward other members of the group, especially the leader.

At a later time in this text, the subject of problem members and how they can be handled will be discussed. For the present, suffice it to be noted that some groups will have difficulty finding cohesiveness. It is the leader's responsibility to discover the cause or causes and attempt to eliminate the hindrances.

In this respect, the leader must also guard against the possibility of playing favorites among the members of the group. It is very easy for the group to get the impression that the leader is protecting one member out of favoritism resulting in the group forming sides such as those who are with the leader, and those who are against him.

6. The leader is responsible for shaping the group into a therapeutic social system. A code of behavior, rules and norms must be established that will guide the interaction of the group. Some actual rules and suggestions for a code of behavior will be discussed later. The importance of this phase of Group Therapy cannot be overemphasized. It was this lack of setting a standard or code of behavior that was essentially the downfall of the Encounter Groups. If the group is conducted on a "no holds barred" basis, someone is likely to get hurt, if not physically then emotionally. The same principles that make for good therapy in a personal counseling session apply to the group. The more decently and in order things are done, the more the group will move confidently toward healing.

7. The leader is also the group expert. At times there will be a need for a technical approach to a particular problem, and the leader must be able to handle such problems. A group leader should have all the training possible before attempting to lead a group. He or she should also be well read on many other subjects in the field of psychology and spirituality. The facilitator need not be an expert in all topics, but well-informed in those areas in which he is expected to be well-informed. However, there is another danger in this area. The leader must not present himself or herself as being completely knowledgeable in all areas of life. No one really likes a know-it-all, especially if the know-it-all is really less informed than he appears to be.

Probably, the most destructive kind of group leader is the "Bible thumper" who has a scripture verse for every problem that is presented. When people find the courage to finally share their most intimate feelings, they need understanding and empathy, not judgment and a pat Bible verse answer. This is not to say that the eventual answer or solution to an individual's problem is not to be found in scripture, but it is important for the group (and the facilitator) to take time to understand and empathize with the persons feelings and perceptions so that when a Bible scripture or

Bible principle is finally offered, it will have real significance. There are times when a group member will present a problem that is in fact only a secondary problem that is not as threatening as the real issue. Often group members will share a problem of concern in order to get a reaction from the rest of the group. If the reaction is one of care and empathy, the individual may find it easier to share the deeper emotional problem at a later time in the session.

8. The leader will shape norms not only through explicit or implicit social engineering, but through the example in the leader's own behavior. Many group members will take the lead of the group facilitator. There are individuals who will even go so far as to imitate the leader. If the leader sets a good example of behavior, group members for the most part will tend to follow their example. If the leader is very open and transparent with the group, the other members will find it a lot easier to become open and the dynamic of self-disclosure will come into play at a much earlier stage in the group. This is particularly true in the case of transference and counter-transference. If the leader reacts to a member of the group in a defensive manner when the member is responding to the leader, as a matter of transference, the rest of the group may assume the reaction is acceptable in this type of therapy. If, however, the leader reacts in a manner that is one of understanding, (not condescending) of the fact that he (the leader) is not the true target, the leader will understand that the member is transferring feelings that are toward another onto the facilitator.

As an elementary school teacher, I learned very early that a student, who behaved angrily towards me in the early morning, was merely transferring his or her feelings of anger or frustration as a result of a family quarrel. It was safer to be angry with me than to argue or rebel against a member of his or her family.

9. The leader must help the group to begin assuming responsibility for its own functioning. The group leader should actually encourage others in the group to assume leadership from time to time. As the members begin to learn how to hear beyond the actual words that are being spoken, they should feel free to ask

or probe statements made by others. All of the questions regarding the clarification of an individual's feelings or thoughts should not come from the leader. There should be a time in a good group where the group can function with or without the official leader being present. Although members in a group are primarily interested in dealing with items of their own agenda, they need to be allowed to also learn how to understand and share in the agendas of others. One of the criticisms of some modern psychologists is that they may tend to keep the client dependent on the therapy (at least as long as the insurance lasts). One of the goals of Christian counseling in general should be to help the counselee (or group member) become able to cope with life's problems and to learn to direct their dependence toward the Lord Jesus Christ.

10. The leader is a facilitator in that they must facilitate self-disclosure which is an absolute essential in the group's therapeutic process.

A. Members will not benefit from group therapy unless they self-disclose and do so fully. This is not to say that a group member must share all of the deep dark secrets of his or her heart. This type of confession is best made to the Lord. "If we confess our sins, he is faithful and just and will forgive us our sins and purify us from all unrighteousness." (I John 1:9, NIV).

B. Self-disclosure should come at the individual's own pace and not be forced. At times certain eager members will try to rush the process of Group Dynamics. Experienced group members (those who have been in groups before) may become impatient with new group members. The leader is responsible to ascertain that the more timid members of the group are given sufficient time to share. There are times when one or more members of the group will never be able to open up to the group about anything but some very unimportant disclosures. Occasionally, a leader will need to ask a member to leave the group because of their inability to share. This, of course, would not be done until the leader is sure beyond a reasonable doubt that there is no hope of any level of disclosure.

Persons who fall into this category may be schizoid and completely unable to share in this way.

C. The group must not be seen as a forced confessional where deep revelations are forced from members one by one. An individual that is pressured to "confess" before he or she is ready, may either lie (as a defense mechanism) or more often simply "clam up" and refuse to say anything. Self-disclosure must be on a "willingness to share" basis. Timing is crucial in Group Therapy. The group leader must be ready and willing to step in and suggest that the sharer be given a little more time before sharing. This is not to say that the leader should become a "savior" figure always trying to spare the feelings of certain members of the group. There will be times in a group that a member will want to self-disclose a feeling or problem that will come too close to a problem that the leader has not completely resolved in his own life. The tendency at such a time may be for the leader to avoid the emotional pain by rescuing the member from the pressure of the group to self-disclose. Group leaders must be willing to examine themselves when confronted with the need to intervene.

D. Self-disclosure is always an interpersonal act. The disclosure must be in the context of a relationship to others. It is important that the members of the group are made aware of the need to listen to other members of the group. An individual who "bares his soul" and is ignored by the group, may suffer considerable emotional pain and actually withdraw into his or her own shell. Each member of the group must share in not only the words that are shared by another member, but they must become aware of the feelings and emotions involved in the self-disclosure. Every self-disclosure must be responded to by the other members of the group.

E. Self-disclosure can serve as a genuine catharsis. At times self-disclosure will almost be a casual interaction between members of the group. The group leader must always be alert to the potential for catharsis in a self-disclosure. There will be times when the leader, if not one of the other members, will need to remind the group that a self-disclosure was not given proper attention and reaction. The word catharsis carries the meaning of cleansing (or healing). A self-disclosure that is correctly handled in the group may not only lead to a healing or cleansing for the group member who is disclosing, but also for others in the group who have been experiencing the same type of problem in their lives. Catharsis can occur as a result of many experiences such as the viewing of a tragic play or listening to a moving piece of music. The atmosphere of the small group tends to produce a catharsis in members of the group through the interpersonal and loving relationships that are characteristic of a good group. Catharsis is not something that can be planned, it just happens in the right emotional environment.

Figure 1, stage 3 on page 62 presents a list of the types of disclosures that can be expected in a typical group. This is important for the group members to understand, and it is very important for the facilitator to monitor. The facilitator and the group must learn a degree of patience with each other. Some areas of feelings will never be shared in the group setting. These feelings will only be dealt with in personal one-on-one counseling if they are ever shared. The facilitator must know and teach the group when to probe and when to permit the individual member to withhold. There are times in a group when the facilitator will need to trust the sensitivity (call it intuition or discernment if you will) of one or more of the members of the group. The following example may illustrate this point.

In a Christian Growth Group that I was facilitating, there was a young man by the name of Phil. Phil was a high school senior, a very good student, and seemed to have a fairly good life. He was a quiet boy, and he was friendly to everyone. It wasn't apparent to me or most of the other people in our fellowship that he was experiencing any serious problems. The group on this particular evening was not very animated. A few people shared rather insignificant problems that the group responded to, but by and large the evening was uneventful. About 15 minutes before the closing time, I suggested that for whatever reason the group was not in the mood for much interaction, and that we might as well dismiss for the evening and take up again next week.

I was interrupted by one of the members of the group. Ruth said, "Doctor Bohac, I feel that there is something bothering Phil, and maybe we need to pray for him and see if he wants to share." I had no objections, so we gathered around Phil and prayed for him. After only a few minutes of prayer, Ruth asked Phil if there was anything he wanted to share. Phil. with some tears, said, "I have been sitting here all evening thinking how I was going to go home and end my life after the session. I was trying to image how I was going to do the job." After this, Phil went on to share the reasons for his despair, and the group ministered to him. I believe that Ruth's discernment actually saved Phil's life that night. As the facilitator, I realized the importance of being willing to yield to the leading of God as He chooses to use another member of the group in a life threatening situation.

There has been considerable research in Group Dynamics to understand the nature and impact of group leaders. Studies indicate that the necessary abilities and skills for effective leadership depend largely on the context in which group interaction occurs (Fiedler, 1964). "Contingency theory" has provided one of the most influential models of leadership effectiveness. Fiedler suggests that in most cases persons adopt one of two leadership styles. Some leaders are task oriented — i.e. they are primarily concerned with getting the job done; others are relationship oriented, focusing first of all on the social-emotional climate of the group (Benner, 1985).

When the group is organized for the purpose of achieving some specific task, the task leader is most likely to achieve the goal with the least effort. However, when the goal of the group is concerned with interpersonal relationships, the self-disclosure may, if given the right atmosphere, lead to what is known in psychology as transference.

Transference is a vital factor in both individual and group therapy. Transference is a psychological condition between two individuals (in the group usually between the member and the facilitator, but not always). When a person is able to relate himself to another person, the relationship is thought of as transference (Bonner, 1959). The term means literally to convey information or content from one person, place, or situation to another. The psychological usage expresses a special type of relationship with another person. The usual pattern is for a person in the present to be experienced as though he or she were a person in the past. Thus transference, at least from the psychoanalytic point of view, is basically a repetition of an old object relationship in which attitudes and feelings, either positive or negative, pertaining to a former relationship have been shifted to a new person in the present. Often a mode of perceiving and responding to the world that was developed in childhood is inappropriately transferred into the adult context (Peck, 1978).

In the broad definition of the term, transference takes place in all relationships to some degree. Everyone has met someone whom they disliked or distrusted immediately for no apparent reason. However, in the counseling situation, whether individual or group, the transference allows for a healing process to occur. Although some psychologists feel that transference is not vital to therapy, the vast majority would agree that transference is the sine qua non of dynamic psychotherapy in that it gives the opportunity to deal with unresolved conflicts of the past.

Jung (1968) saw transference as a special case of projection, a psychological mechanism that carries over subjective contents from both the personal unconscious (shadows) and the collective unconscious (archetypes) to the object of the therapist (or in the group to the facilitator or another member of the group). He further maintained that transference was neither voluntary nor intentional. It takes place spontaneously and without provocation. This is especially true in the group counseling setting.

Researchers from the behavioral orientation suggest that transference is a special form of generalized learning. The therapist provides the social situation much like those in which the patient has previously been punished or rewarded by significant others. The stimulus of the therapist, or the facilitator, or another member of the group, provokes the same responses that the person learned in an earlier relationship. Benner (1985) concludes that transference is seen as involving genuine fear and new feelings for the therapist that are generalized by the person from previous learning conditions.

Meier, et. al. (1991) gives the following definition for transference as: the patient's unconscious disproportionate emotional response to the therapist. In the counseling group the target may be the facilitator or another member of the group. Occasionally, in the group setting an individual may express transference against the entire group. At first, the outburst may sound like an honest frustration with the group progress. However, the patient facilitator will be able to recognize the situations as a transfer of childhood experience with grown-ups who either did not take the time to listen to the plight of the youngster or reacted negatively to the cry for help.

I was conducting one of several Encounter Groups while in training at the University. The group included a number of individuals who had apparently been in groups before. The group was to meet on Friday evening, all day on Saturday until 10:00pm, and half of Sunday, because it was a Training Group.

I had decided that I would experiment with a new technique. As the group gathered, I took my place among them without any introduction to the group of my role as the facilitator. It did not take them long to find me out. Someone asked why we weren't doing something. I asked what he wanted to do. His response was that we should engage in some type of role playing or some sort of game (in Gestalt psychology it was believed that the way to get in touch with feelings was to engage in various physical activities.) I suggested that if the group wanted to play some games in order to get in touch with their feelings that I would not object, but that I was not particularly enamored with Gestalt theory.

Several of the individuals began to attack me verbally suggesting that I was a very poor excuse for a facilitator and that I was insensitive to their needs. I will discuss more about this group in another place in this text. Through this process of transference of frustration, I learned a great deal about many of the group's members. First of all, they had all had previous experience in groups, and they were well-informed as to how a group and the facilitator in particular should function. Second, I was aware that many of the group members had been in therapy over the years and were well-acquainted with the theories and concepts of the various popular treatment modalities. Third but not last, I became aware that many of the members of this particular group had issues of being disappointed with others that they looked to for help and guidance."

THE GROUP FACILITATOR AS A STUDENT OF HUMAN BEHAVIOR

An effective facilitator will have a good understanding of human behavior. There are numerous ways that the leader can determine what is going on in a particular member of a group. Here are a few techniques that will give the leader clues of what is happening in the members:

BODY LANGUAGE

Much can be learned about an individual's feelings by certain body clues. A person who looks straight into the eyes of the person who is speaking may have genuine regard for the person, while a person who habitually avoids eye contact may be expressing dislike or fear (Bates and Johnson, 1972). Non-verbal signals can tell more than verbal ones if the observer is aware of what is happening physically. In a relationship involving a speaker and several listeners, such as a classroom, the speaker can be fairly certain that the individual who is sitting with arms folded across his chest is resisting what is being said. On the other hand, a listener who listens with his mouth partly open probably wants to take in everything that is being said.

Bates and Johnson (1972) also note that leaders need to be alert to any changes in posture. One of the most common examples is the person who fidgets, changing his posture frequently. Other messages of silence include the shifting of the eyes from place to place but seldom toward the speaker. The leader needs to store this information away for possible use in the future. It should be noted that individuals respond to other members of the group through body language as well.

There are times when the leader may wish to do a little teaching on this topic to help the rest of the group become aware of each other's responses or lack thereof.

Body language is the language spoken by the body as a whole or in part, and usually without the awareness of the person involved. There are several members of the body that are particularly active in body language.

HANDS AND FEET

Bates and Johnson (1972) suggest that "the thumbs tightly enclosed within the fist may suggest to group leaders to proceed with caution, while a member who has both thumbs within his fists sends an even stronger 'red flag' message." They also suggest that a person sitting with the hands in a 'palms up' position may suggest a willingness to receive a message. Hands over the mouth may indicate a desire to communicate coupled with some hesitancy to do so. Inner tensions may well be indicated by the twirling of a ring on the finger.

The group leader needs to be alert to all of these physical acts as possible indicators of inner tensions, anxiety, anger, or any number of emotions. However, caution must be exercised not to read too much into some body behaviors. The member's nose may actually be itching.

THE FACE

Mehrabian (1968) showed that facial expressions conveyed over 55 percent of the meaning of a message. Group leaders can learn much (and teach the group in turn) about what is happening by observing those "complex yet fleeting messages that the face expresses" (Bates and Johnson, 1972).

The eyes, perhaps more than other facial features, are the most expressive. It is not possible, of course, to tell everything that the eyes may be saying, but the presence of a tear, or a frown, or perhaps a vacant stare, can speak volumes. Closed eyes or the absence of eye contact can indicate an inner struggle or a resistance to what is being said. Very rapid eye movement is an indication of the presence of anxiety or guilt feelings. This same rapid eye movement may indicate a search for an exit (Bates and Johnson, 1972).

Bates and Johnson (1972) suggest that the "smile which is not in harmony with a verbal message is usually quite apparent, as is the self-abnegating laugh, the nervous giggle, or the clearing of the throat." They also note that the voice in general can portray an image other than intended. A voice that is whining in nature or one that resembles the voice of a little boy or girl may be indicative of an unconscious cry for the tender understanding of a caring mother. One of the most effective ways of tuning into the voices of the group is to listen to a tape of the group session. Care must be taken to assure the group members that the tape will only be used by the leader to evaluate the session.

Messages that are non-verbal cannot be read with absolute certainty. The leader must not read too much into these messages. It is possible, for example that a group member may be suffering from an abscessed tooth. The look of pain on his or her face has nothing to do with what is happening in the group, nor does it reflect any feelings of rejection toward the leader. At times, it is perfectly acceptable and proper for the leader to simply ask the individual if he or she is in physical pain. It would be better to suggest an aspirin for the pain, than to go on for hours wondering what the facial expressions were representing.

BODY POSTURE

Another source of non-verbal information is body posturing. The individual who leans into the group is showing a certain amount of genuine interest, while the individual who slumps or leans away from the group, is giving an entirely different message.

Eric Berne (1961) suggests that, "body stance communicates information concerning which of the three (parent, child, or adult) ego states is in control at any given time." A counselor who expects to conduct groups on a regular basis should become familiar with the work of Berne. Body language messages are sent in many different ways. Drastic changes in mode of dress may indicate a change of attitude toward the group as a whole or toward the leader in particular (Bates and Johnson, 1972).

TERRITORIALITY

Bates and Johnson (1972) indicate that there is an invisible line (or circle) around each person that defines his or her life space. With many people this line is very near to them and others can come close without creating any anxiety. Other people have a territorial line that is further away, and anyone who gets too close will trigger an anxiety response.

Many years ago, I read about a research project that was done at a penitentiary. The subjects were men who had committed crimes ranging from simple assault to premeditated murder. The subjects were placed individually in a chair in a sound-proof room and blindfolded. Each subject in turn was connected to a polygraph that would measure changes in pulse, breathing and secretion of perspiration that would indicate agitation or anxiety in the subject. Around the chair in the middle of the room there were drawn concentric circles, each one a little farther from the subject. A number of researchers were then allowed to quietly enter the room in their stocking feet so that the subject could not hear any sound betraying the distance that the researcher was from the subject. Each concentric circle was given a rated number and each subject was rated as to the level or severity of his aggressiveness. The study showed that the individual with the highest level of aggressiveness was able to detect the presence of a person in the room at a much greater distance than those with milder aggressiveness levels. The findings of the study suggested that certain people have a broader range of territorial space than others.

One of the Gestalt games often used in the group is the territorial game. Members of the group are asked to sit in a fairly close circle. They are told to close their eyes, raise their arms and wave them around to explore the space around them. After a time, the leader will ask the group to share their feelings during this game. A number of the members of the group will almost always indicate that they felt someone else's hand touch theirs and felt a little (or a lot) resentful of the intrusion into their space. Considerable research has been done to verify that people in general can be separated into "touch and no touch" personalities. Some people enjoy touching and being touched while others do not. People usually do not fall entirely into one group or the other but somewhere on a continuum between the two extremes.

NON-VERBAL EXERCISES AND BODY LANGUAGE EXERCISES

In the tradition of the Gestalt theorist, there are a number of exercises that can be used to help the group learn more about these non-verbal languages. This text will not go into great detail in discussing them, but the potential group leader would do well to take the time to investigate some of the possibilities. Listed here are only a few, with a very short introduction to each.

EYE CONTACT

Have the group divide into twos. Have the members of each couple try to communicate to his or her partner with the eyes only. The partner is to try to understand what the other is trying to say.

TRANSMITTING EMOTIONS

Again with members divided into couples they are told to try and express emotions (anger, anxiety, love, fear, etc.) in non-verbal terms. As a variation of this exercise, the members are told to wear masks to cover their faces and again attempt to communicate emotions or feelings.

There are many others. The book by Bates and Johnson (1972) is an excellent source for some more of these. In the chapter on conducting a group, there will be several suggestions for other techniques that can help people get in touch with their feelings. These exercises can bring an awareness of the importance of non-verbal language.

CO-LEADER

Research is scarce on the use of a co-facilitator. There are several reasons why a co-leader may be advisable. The main consideration, of course, is the strength and confidence of the leader himself. A leader, having even a slight problem with self-esteem, may find it difficult to share the position of leadership with another. A co-leader is especially advisable when the leader himself may not have much experience in leading groups. The following suggestions may be helpful when selecting a successful co-leader:

1. If at all possible, choose a friend rather than a stranger. The co-leader should be someone in whom the leader has confidence. Choosing a stranger can present problems, since the individual may not be stable enough to withstand the stress and pressure in a group situation.

2. It is wise to choose a person whose psychological and spiritual orientation is similar to that of the leader. Disagreements over psychological or religious beliefs can, and most certainly will, prove to be a disrupting factor in the group. It is not necessary that both leaders believe everything alike, but the closer the two leaders are, the greater the possibility of success. The most desirable

situation would be one in which the two leaders could assume an equal status as leaders of the group. This would not be possible in a case where the pastor is the leader and a lay person was to assume the co-leader position.

3. In a mixed group of males and females, it is advisable to select a co-leader of the opposite sex. This will assure a greater understanding of both male and female points of view. Some theorists believe that it is not necessary to select a co-leader of the opposite sex.

4. It would be advisable to select a co-leader with a similar leadership style. If the leaders do not have a similar leadership styles they could create considerable confusion in the group, and this most likely would destroy any possibility of cohesiveness.

It is important to note at this juncture that there are many potential problems that can arise in the group as a consequence of the interpersonal relations of the leaders. The members of the group may divide their loyalty between the two leaders. This would destroy the goals of the group and may even cause severe damage to some of the more emotionally frail members of the group.

This is not to say that the two leaders must always agree completely. It is hoped that the two facilitators would each be able to function as just another member of the group. The proper kind of interaction in disagreement can be an important social learning tool for others in the group.

If two therapists work together for a period of time, they will develop the ability to know when to disagree and how that disagreement is to be handled. They will also develop a system of non-verbal and subtle-verbal clues to indicate to each other any concern over a possible situation developing that could be harmful to the health of the group. It is to be hoped that the two leaders could agree beforehand, that if they find it too difficult to work productively together, that one or the other will graciously withdraw without causing any disruption in the group. Anyone working with people in counseling whether in groups or in private sessions must adopt the dictum of medicine: Do no harm!

"Success is not final, failure is not fatal: it is the courage to continue that counts."

- Winston Churchill

CHAPTER 4:

ORGANIZING A CHRISTIAN SMALL GROUP

Getting a group together is not the difficult part. In most churches, there will be many people who will welcome the opportunity to participate in a group, especially if they think that there is a chance that they will receive healing or at least help. The difficult part is in making sure that the group is going to be a success. Griffin (1982) paraphrases the rhyme about the little girl with a curl: "When groups are good, they are very, very good. And when they are bad, they are horrid."

IMPORTANT ELEMENTS IN GROUP MINISTRY

When forming a group, there are several elements to consider. The following material is intended for the Christian Growth Groups in particular. Most of the suggestions would also apply to other types of groups as well.

THE MAKE-UP OF THE GROUP

The first question to be answered when planning a group is the question of Heterogeneity versus Homogeneity: In this case the choice is not with regard to the sex of the individuals. In most groups it is advisable to have both males and females together. There are times, of course, when a group consisting of men (or women) only, would be advisable. This is particularly true if the group is a care group for widowers, for example. It has been demonstrated that a homogeneous group with respect to similarity of problems or needs tends to gain a sense of cohesiveness more quickly. There are however, some limitations to the homogeneous group. The more people are alike, the more limited will be their interaction over the long haul. The Heterogeneous group with people of different ages, sex, marital status, socio-economic status, level of spirituality, etc. have, according to Dibbert and Wichem (1985), some real advantages. The advantages include: the opportunity to learn to empathize and understand others who are different in some way, members can learn more about life and its challenges, etc. It is important to note that a group that is too different can also present problems. Very old people in a group of very young people can present a disastrous situation. Many older people have problems remembering the difficulties of adolescence. Older people who are better informed, and who have been able to keep pace with the changes that have occurred with regards to the younger generation, can serve to assist in the bridging of the generation gap.

The next step to starting a group is to decide exactly what type of group will be organized. As stated above, most of the emphasis of this book will be on the organization and performance of a Christian Growth Group, but there are many other types of groups that can be organized to help people in need. A listing of the various types of groups was included in an earlier chapter. There are certain elements that are common to the organization of any type of group.

Once it has been determined what type of group is to be organized, the following matters should be carefully considered to insure the success of the group.

WHO WILL BE OFFERED THE OPPORTUNITY OF JOINING THE GROUP?

In the case of a Christian Growth Group, it is fairly safe to make a general announcement to an entire population such as a church. It may be necessary to limit the group because of too many people indicating an interest. There are also a few people who should be asked not to participate.

PEOPLE THAT SHOULD BE EXCLUDED FROM THE GROUP:

People who are too busy to attend every session.

Continuity is a very important factor in the success of any group. Members need to be informed of the importance of faithful attendance to every session, except in the case of a dire emergency, of course. Faithfulness should not be presented as a kind of arbitrary rule, but faithful attendance should be made a condition for membership on the basis of it being a Christian virtue. The group leader must use great wisdom in determining whether a member misses meetings for good reasons. If certain individuals are habitually truant, the rest of the group will begin to show resentment.

People who really aren't interested.

Some people may agree to attend because they were pressured by a spouse, a parent, or a friend. Occasionally, an individual will sign-up for a group because of a court order or as a condition of parole. These people often make fairly good group members, because even though they may resent having to attend, they also realize the consequences of missing or dropping out. The decision on admitting these individuals into the group must be made by the leader after a conference with the person to determine their ability to profit from a group experience.

Persons who will not be able to keep what they hear confidential.

Occasionally a person may need to be excluded from a group because they are only interested in the group as a source of gossip. Nothing will destroy a group faster than having a "snitch" in the group.

Ida was in her late 60's at the time she indicated her desire to join a Christian Growth Group that I was leading. Against my better judgment, I permitted her to join. It was not because of her age that I had some doubts; it was due to the feeling I had that she was not bright enough to gain from the group experience. There was no doubt that Ida possessed a limited intelligence. Her husband had died two year before, and I felt reasonably sure that she had not completely gotten over his death. She was well known in the Christian fellowship at Logos, and some of the other people also wondered about the advisability of allowing her into the group. She was a rather frail, pathetic individual. She could not have weighed more than 70 pounds. She was usually dirty and unkempt, and it was some of these features that prompted me to allow her to participate. Ida sat through each of the first few sessions without saying a word. A few people tried to draw her into the conversation, but she sat stoically by while others shared some of their problems cautiously. Needless to say, the group was not developing as it should. Then, several of the other members complained to me that Ida was sharing everything she heard in the group with her circle of friends. I had to ask Ida not to come back to the group. She was devastated, and with many tears swore that she had not shared anything with anyone.

After Ida left the group, the group soon grew in self-disclosure, and some very wonderful healings took place. A group leader must be very careful to protect the confidentiality of the group. This group could have been completely destroyed.

Persons who are known to have a serious emotional or mental problem.

Later in this text, the author will discuss several testing materials that are not only effective in "weeding out" certain persons who are a risk in this type of group but can also serve as a means of getting the group into serious discussions about their own personality needs. In the case of persons with serious emotional problems or even borderline mental problems, the group leader would be well-advised to refer them to a more thoroughly qualified counselor. It is only in the controlled setting of a psychiatric hospital or other such institution that some individuals would be considered "safe." It is because such psychotics may not be in touch with reality that they are not candidates for Christian Growth

Groups or most other groups that would be led by even a well-trained Christian Counselor.

There will be times when an individual will get into the group without the leader being aware of the severity of a serious psychological problem. For this reason, it is always wise to have a licensed psychologist or psychiatrist available who may be called in the case of an emergency. There are times, when a group is made up of strong Christians, and a case of serious disturbance can be handled by prayer or even exorcism. It is, however, strongly suggested that such things as exorcism only be considered by leadership with considerable experience in this type of ministry.

Persons under the care of a psychologist.

If a person is known to be under the care of a psychologist or other mental health person, the leader should contact that person and discuss the possibility of including their client in the group. Psychologists, and even medical doctors, will often refer people to a group. In such a case, the leader has a responsibility to provide the referring person with any important information gained through the group. This of course, would be with the client's permission and knowledge. Professional ethics would suggest that the group leader has a responsibility not to breach the professional relationship that exists between two health care people. Maintaining good relationships with other health care professionals may very well result in referrals for future groups.

Extremely hostile people.

Occasionally, an individual will appear to be very hostile or have a history of extremely aggressive behavior that may not show on a personality test. If it is known to the leader that this is true of a person who is indicating an interest in the group, it would be prudent to refer such a person to individual counseling, rather than the group. Over a period of time, the aggressive person may gain enough help from individual counseling to be allowed to participate in a group. Occasionally, a person who is very hostile will join a group without the leader being aware of the level of hostility. The leader must always be ready to deal with emergencies that may arise from the explosion of a very hostile person. If at all possible, the group leader should have a working relationship with a licensed psychologist who could be called in case of such an emergency. This is one area in which the MMPI (Minnesota Multiphasic Personality Inventory) can be of real help. If the leader finds from the individual profiles, that one person scores very high in hostility, good sense dictates that the individual be excluded from the group and referred to a counselor for individual counseling.

OPEN VERSUS CLOSED GROUPS

The open group allows for new members to join whenever members leave. The closed group is one that does not allow new members to join. Open groups may go on indefinitely, while the closed group will usually have a set number of meetings. People, who wish to join a closed group that is in progress, can be told that they will be able to join the next group that will commence after the present group completes its predetermined series of meetings.

Both types of groups have advantages and disadvantages. The open group allows for "new blood" to bring some sense of refreshing to the group from time to time, however, whenever a new person joins the group, it should be expected that the rest of the group will need time to build trust in the newcomer.

The closed group can become very cohesive, but if some members drop out the group may become too small to be effective. Whether the group is opened or closed, the leader should allow the rest of the members to decide whether a new member should be allowed to join the group. The group should also have a say in who the new member will be.

SETTING THE RULES FOR A NEW GROUP

Not only is it important to set certain norms and rules for a new group, it is also important that the norms and rules be reviewed from time to time. The following represents the most important rules. Occasionally, others will need to be added.

1. Attendance is important. Members must commit themselves to make every effort to attend every meeting possible. In addition to the fact that other members of a group will resent members who miss group meetings, there is the fact that continuity of the group process can only happen when all of the members are faithful in attendance. The discussion of this rule with the group may take on the metaphor of medical model. A patient must be faithful in treatment or the treatment will not have its desired effect. There may well be times when a particular member of the group will need to miss a session for a very good reason. This should be taken into account. It is the member who makes a habit of missing who needs to be asked to drop out and perhaps join another group at a later date when they will not be so busy.

2. Self-disclosure is a MUST: Members will be expected to be an active part of the group. No spectators are allowed. It is only when the members of the group feel safe and confident in the sincerity of the rest of the group that any real self-disclosure will take place. A group leader must realize the importance of self-disclosure. If there is the slightest concern about such things as confidentiality, or the possibility of rejection by the leader or members of the group, no member is going to bare his own soul through self-disclosure. The group will consequently result in an exercise in futility with members becoming more and more inclined to drop out. The justification for group therapy is the creation of a safe, non-judgmental, loving atmosphere in which a person can feel free to share those things that are at the root of his or her emotional problems. This principle is based on solid Biblical teaching as found in the book of James:

> *"Therefore confess your sins to each other and pray*
> *for each other so that you maybe healed. The prayer*
> *of a righteous man is powerful and effective."*
> *James 5:16, NIV.*

The King James Version uses the word "faults" instead of sins, but the meaning is the same. God has provided for man a simple, but effective way of dealing with faults or sins. The key, of course, is the prayer for one another.

3. Labeling will not be allowed (as noted in an earlier section of this text): Members must refrain from using labels in referring to the behavior or comments of another member. The leader must take the initiative by avoiding the use of psychological terminology with reference to behavior, and at the same time teach, as unobtrusively as possible, the importance of avoiding the use of labels. An individual who is experiencing a problem with fear must not be labeled as being "paranoid?" There are many other examples that could be given. The simplest solution is to simply avoid, and encourage members to avoid, such terms as "manic-depressive, schizophrenia, anxiety reaction, hypochondriacal reaction, asthenia reaction, etc." Even such apparently harmless terms as "lazy" "cold" or "unfeeling" can be very hurtful to certain individuals. The group must learn to listen to what is behind the words of a member of the group before forming any preconceived notion of some personality problem that characterizes the person. It is often what is not being said that is more important than what is being said.

In the past few years, there has been a great deal of interest in the personality typing introduced by Rev. Tim LaHaye. His short, somewhat unscientific book on temperament theory has resulted in other psychologically oriented Christian theorists to further develop the concepts of personality temperament. This author would discourage the use of the terms of personality theory in the group for the same reasons that other forms of labeling are not conducive to good group therapy. Individuals must not be allowed to hide behind the concept (or label of) melancholic, or choleric, etc. in order to escape dealing with certain emotional problems or personality faults.

4. Verbal or physical attack will not be permitted. Verbal attacks can be as painful as, or actually more devastating than, an actual physical attack. Neither physical nor verbal attacks can ever

be permitted in a group setting. The earlier forms of Encounter Groups used the verbal attack method of confrontation as a means of "breaking down" the defenses of members of the group. There was much support for this method of stimulating involvement, but this type of confrontation is not considered as acceptable in a Christian Growth Group. The leader (mental health care worker) who may wish to conduct an Encounter Group should be specially trained to deal with the problems that may, and do, occur in such groups. If the attack is the result of true transference, the leader must be able to skillfully handle the process and allow for some latitude for this expression of repressed feelings so that true catharsis may take place. In this type of "explosion" of feeling, the leader can help the rest of the group to better understand the process of transference. Transference can be a very healthy release of repressed feeling that will ultimately result in healing.

5. Members should be expected to do whatever assignments are given as part of the group's activities (bible reading, prayer, etc.). The Christian Growth Group is intended to be a therapy group, but as a part of that therapy each member is expected to complete certain assignments each week. The following are the types of assignments that are very helpful:

A. Each member is asked to read a specific portion of the Bible. The most effective Bible reading would be a short passage that is read over each day for the entire week. Members should not be asked if they did the reading, but the leader should remind the members each week of the importance of the activity. It goes without saying that the portion of Scripture that is chosen to be read each week should be one that has significant teachings related to the goals of the group. A few scriptures that have been used with great success are:

Ephesians 1:3-14. The members are asked to personalize the verses in the following manner:

> "*Blessed be the God and Father of our Lord Jesus Christ, who has blessed us with every spiritual*

blessing in the heavenly places in Christ, just as He chose us in Him before the foundation of the world, that we would be holy and blameless before Him. In love He predestined us to adoption as sons through Jesus Christ to Himself, according to the kind intention of His will, to the praise of the glory of His grace, which He freely bestowed on us in the Beloved. In Him we have redemption through His blood, the forgiveness of our trespasses, according to the riches of His grace which He lavished on us. In all wisdom and insight He made known to us the mystery of His will, according to His kind intention which He purposed in Him with a view to an administration suitable to the fullness of the times, that is, the summing up of all things in Christ, things in the heavens and things on the earth. In Him also we have obtained an inheritance, having been predestined according to His purpose who works all things after the counsel of His will, to the end that we who were the first to hope in Christ would be to the praise of His glory. In Him, you also, after listening to the message of truth, the gospel of your salvation—having also believed, you were sealed in Him with the Holy Spirit of promise, who is given as a pledge of our inheritance, with a view to the redemption of God's own possession, to the praise of His glory."

The personalizing of scripture can bring great healing and consolation to the members as they begin to understand their position in Christ. Even those members who may not have had a true born-again experience will be thrilled and occasionally, individuals will give their hearts to the Lord as a result of the power of the Word of God applied personally. Other Scriptures will be suggested in Chapter 5.

B. Members are asked to pray for each member of the

group everyday during the week. This is important for the obvious reason that prayer is effective, but praying for one another also helps the members develop a closer emotional connection with the other members of the group. This part of the group requirement cannot be over emphasized. Often, as a result of a member praying for other members, the Lord will reveal some truth concerning a particular member. This is not inconsistent with the teaching of the Word about spiritual gifts.

C. Each member is asked to read a chapter of a good Christian book that has been selected to fit the particular needs of the group. For example, a marriage enrichment group may be asked to read a chapter of the book by Cecil Osborn, *The Art of Understanding Your Mate* on a weekly basis. A group of younger, unmarried adults may be assigned the book, *The Art of Understanding Yourself* by the same author. A very fine book to be used for a mixed group, whose goal is emotional healing, would be a volume by Parker entitled, *The Power of Prayer*. Some other titles will be listed in the Bibliography.

6. Complete confidentiality is mandatory. Every good text book on counseling, whether group or individual, will make several references to the importance of confidentiality. Members should be warned that if anyone in the group breaks the rule of confidentiality, they will immediately be asked to leave the group. This can be done firmly but with love. This rule of confidentiality is to be observed even between husband and wife. The husband may not be given to gossip, but the wife may. Read again the section on "Persons That Should Be Excluded from the Group" on page 86.

A few weeks before the group is to start, it is advisable to have each prospective member complete a special personality inventory test. There are a number of these tests available. The Minnesota Multiphasic Personality Inventory (MMPI) is a good test to be used by a leader who has some training in personality assessment. The Yokefellow groups use this test. The members take the test, and it is sent to the offices of the Yokefellows Counseling Center for scoring and evaluation. Each member will receive an evaluation slip every two weeks from the center. The slip will explain, in clear terms, the particular phase of personality that was tested, with some suggestions about ways of gaining help for any problems the members may be having in that area. The slip will also include some Bible reading to help the member change any undesirable personality traits.

Another fine test is the one that is found in the Personality Self-Portrait, by Oldham. This is a self-administered, self-scored test. There are thirteen areas of personality that are evaluated. The group using this device will find a lot of interesting discussion that will center on each member sharing their own score. Such personality characteristics as "vigilant, solitary, idiosyncratic, self-confident, etc." are explored. The leader should ask to see all of the plotted graphs for the members of the group. A member scoring very high on the "L" area of the test could perceive himself or herself as being very aggressive and may present some problems in the group. This is also true of a high score in area "H" indicating that the individual is very sensitive. Sensitivity is a desirable trait as a rule, but one who is overly sensitive will need to be watched, as this person would tend to become hurt very easily by even a casual, innocent comment by the leader or a fellow member of the group.

Another test that can be very valuable in assessing areas of personality that may be troublesome to individuals is the Millon (1981) Personality Inventory. Theodore Millon was a major contributor to the DSM III guide to personality disorders. The Personality Inventory would indicate more than others, except for the MMPI, those individuals who would best be excluded from the group and recommended for personal therapy.

Setting the day and time: The day and time of the meetings can be of special importance. The meetings should not interfere with other activities of the church. This can only lead to conflict and most likely a failed group. The meeting day should not interfere with special school activities. In smaller towns in the Midwest, Friday evening is traditionally the night for high school football and basketball. The parents of children that are involved in these types of activities should not be asked to attend a group rather than attend their child's school functions.

The time of the meetings must be set so that working people will have enough time to get home from work, eat their supper, and spend a little time with the family. The length of the meeting should be limited to no more than three hours (unless the group meeting is to be a Marathon Group).

The meeting place: The place where the group is to meet is as important as many of the other considerations mentioned. In order to ensure confidentiality, the meeting should take place in a room that is not in or near the center of church activity. The group must feel reasonably certain that they will not be overheard by people in the halls.

The meeting room should be large enough to seat 1-15 people comfortably. The room must be well ventilated so that it will not get stuffy. The temperature in the room must be neither too warm nor too cool. A room that is not a comfortable temperature will result in people becoming distracted by their discomfort. Windows that face the outside of the building on the first floor will create a sense of insecurity, because outsiders will be able to see into the room and possibly hear what is being said. At times the discussion or sharing in a group will become louder than normal conversation, giving the impression to people outside the room that "something strange is going on."

Lighting in the group room should not be overly bright. Most group leaders prefer rather dim lighting, but not so dim as to create the impression of a psychic atmosphere or a feeling of mysticism.

The seating arrangement is also important. Many group leaders prefer having the members sit on the floor on pillows and bean bags facing one another. The reason for this arrangement will become evident in a later discussion of the most helpful methods of communication in a small group. If the room is not too large, members can sit leaning against the wall. Some chairs can become very uncomfortable after an hour or so. Other chairs (the overstuffed variety) can become too comfortable, especially for those group members who have strenuous or stressful work during the day just prior to coming to the meeting.

Many leaders find that classical music played quietly in the background will help the group relax. The leader must follow the lead of the group on whether to use music or not. Some members will find it distracting. If the room is situated in an area where people will be passing by or gathered outside the room for short periods of time, the placement of a stereo speaker just outside the door to the room will mask any discussions from the group inside.

Many groups, especially the "12 Step Groups," will serve coffee and cookies or some other form of refreshments for the members of the group. It is advisable to suggest that the refreshments should be used before the beginning of the group and at a short break in the middle of the session. Some groups would not be disturbed by a member getting up to get refreshments at other times, but there is always the possibility of interrupting a special emotional exchange between members. Again, the leader must sense the will of the group in this.

It is also wise to have a box or two of tissues in the room for those times when a member becomes overwhelmed emotionally. The leader must be aware of the individual (or two) who will always play the role of mother comforter. An individual who is experiencing a real breakthrough emotionally, and who may be weeping almost uncontrollably, should be comforted, but at the right time. It is seldom productive to smother the griever in an attempt to spare them the pain in the moment of grief. Grieving is, in and of itself, healing and must be allowed to take its course.

The first meeting: The first meeting is important because most of the people attending may be a little apprehensive about what is going to happen, especially if they have never been in a group before or have had a bad group experience in the past.

The group leader, assisted by a co-leader, if one is used, should begin the first meeting in prayer and a short worshipful chorus. Someone else can be asked to lead the chorus if the leader does not feel competent. In groups where no one seems adept at leading the singing, the leader may use an audio tape with which the group may sing along.

A member, who has been asked to do so before the meeting, can read a short passage of scripture. There are times when a short piece of inspirational reading may be substituted for the scripture reading, however, even in the non-Christian groups, the Bible will play a very important part in the process of healing.

At this juncture the leader should explain what is about to happen, and what the rules of the meeting will be. It is wise to have the six rules mentioned previously, printed out on a 3 X 5 index card for each of the members. In addition to the individual cards, the leader should have the six rules printed out on a large piece of poster board and hung in a strategic place in the room. The weekly assignments should be given with as much explanation as necessary. This information could also be printed out beforehand to help the members remember.

The leader needs to take the time to answer any questions that the members of the group may have. If a personality profile is used, the leader should give a careful explanation of just what is entailed in the profile. The members need to be assured that they alone will see the results of the profile, and that they will not be pressured to share until they are ready to do so. There are other methods of starting a group. Some of those techniques will be explained in greater detail in Chapter 5.

"Success does not consist in never making mistakes but in never making the same one a second time."

- George Bernard Shaw

CHAPTER 5:

GROUP TECHNIQUES

Any techniques or "games" that are suggested in this chapter should only be used if there is a perceived need to 1) get the group started if there seems to be a hesitance on the part of the members, 2) get the group unstuck, if they seem too bogged down at some point in the process and can't seem to get moving again, 3) deal with specific types of emotional situations that seem to be frustrating the group, and/or 4) teach a particular point that can best be illustrated through interpersonal interaction.

SAY NOTHING AND LET THE SILENCE DO THE WORK

There will be times during one of the group sessions when doing nothing, saying nothing, and letting the silence do the work, will result in a group experience that will be memorable. As a rule, people in a group will become very uneasy when absolutely nothing seems to be happening. It is in these times of silence however, that an interesting Group Dynamic may take place. After a period of silence, some of the members may one by one begin to shift their posture, clear their throats, or actually get up and move about the room. These expressions of uneasiness present the leader with the opportunity to ask the group what they are feeling. Most often the members of the group will begin sharing their opinions or thoughts. It is here that the leader must remind the group that although thoughts and opinions are important to our everyday life, in the group situation the object is to get in touch with feelings. The leader might ask, "John, how did you feel during the time when the entire group was silent?" John may answer, "I wanted to get up and leave. I was so uncomfortable I felt a great deal of anxiety." The next question would be, "Why do you think you felt so uncomfortable?" The answer to that question can open a great deal of dialog and sharing of feelings that the group has not experienced before.

I have used the technique of silence to begin a new Sensitivity Group. I have mentioned the results of this experiment in another place earlier in this book. The result of this type of beginning was an immediate launching into feelings and the expressing of emotions that made the group very exciting and successful. This was a Marathon Group and in Marathon Groups it is always good to get things on the move as soon as possible. If the group is allowed to settle into some lower level of interaction, nothing may happen until the end of the second day. Creating a way to launch a Marathon Group into interaction is completely justified. When I refused to go along with a few of the members who wanted to play games, it added to their frustration. It is not wise to work with a group at this level unless there is someone who is serving as a co-leader or consulting psychologist in the meeting.

USE SOME OF THE GESTALT INTERPERSONAL TECHNIQUES

There are many interaction techniques (games) that can be used to help groups get started or get unstuck. The most effective use of these techniques however, is to make members of the group more sensitive to one another or to help them become more aware of their own true feelings. Each of the following techniques is explained briefly here, but the student who intends to conduct groups should obtain some of the literature on Gestalt psychology in order to become effective in the techniques.

USE ROLE PLAY.

THIS IS USUALLY MORE EFFECTIVE AFTER THE GROUP HAS BEEN MEETING FOR A FEW WEEKS.

Role playing is the rehearsal or recapitulation of an event, real or imagined, with the goal of changing behavior, thinking, and/or feelings (Baker, 1985). Role playing may be used to serve a number of purposes: to help the leader and other members better understand how the individual feels, to help the members of the group make suggestions as to the problem as it appears to them, and as a catalyst for change in the individual. By allowing the member to "play the role of" a father, it will be easier for the person to share his feelings than if he were to be asked to share as himself. One of the advantages of using role play in the group is that the members will be learning a technique they will be able to use in everyday life after the group disbands. Role playing can, and often does, serve to elicit strong, often deeply repressed emotions, and for that reason is potentially very dangerous under the direction of untrained persons. This is especially true if the group is made up of emotionally unstable teenagers. The up side is that the use of role playing can be very therapeutic (Benner, 1985).

ROLE REVERSAL TECHNIQUE

In this technique, the individual "becomes" a significant other. He or she is asked to assume the speech, body posture, mannerisms, and any other qualities unique to the other. The purposes of role reversal are 1) to allow the client to experience the thoughts and feelings of the other; 2) to create an awareness of the consequences of his or her behavior, 3) to assist an auxiliary ego to play the role of the other; 4) to assist the leader or members of the group creating a picture of the individual's conflict (Benner, 1985).

Approach-avoidance exercises Shultz (1967) called the following exercise "the encounter."

Two people are asked to stand at opposite ends of the room. They are instructed to remain silent, look into each other's eyes, and walk very slowly toward each other. Without planning anything, when the two people get close to each other, they are to do whatever they are compelled from within themselves to do (short of physical violence, of course). They are to continue the encounter for as long as they wish. After it is completed, the principals will ordinarily talk about their feelings, and the others will contribute their observations and identifications with the principals. It is essential to urge the principals to try to let their feelings take over and not plan what they will do when they meet. Ohlson (1977) suggests that there are no special problems with this experience. It can be revealing and unsettling, but people usually know whether or not they are ready for it. Anyone who is extremely anxious should not be forced to participate. They may feel more relaxed after watching some of the other members of the group complete the exercise.

This experience is useful in helping to reveal problems when the people are not really aware that a problem exists. Married couples could be involved, but it may be more effective to pair them with someone other than the own mate. Some of the things that may be revealed in this exercise include:

Awareness of one's issues with certain personality types. Coupling a man who may have some problems relating to certain types of women can help bring out the anxiety that he feels in the presence of domineering women, for example.

> A woman's issues with shy men might be revealed in an exercise that couples a strong female with a relatively quiet man.

> A recently divorced man may become aware of his hostility toward women in general and with certain personality types in particular.

Some of the signs of anxiety or hostility are the avoidance of eye contact, change in the body posture, nervous fidgeting with hands, and even signs of giddiness on the part of one or both of the participants. The most valuable information will be gained from the expression of feelings by the two participants. The rest of the group will also be able to make valuable observations as they see things from the perspective of an outsider.

Another psychodrama technique that Shultz suggests is to be used when a member is feeling alienation, isolation, or loneliness in the group. These conditions may come as a result of the leader's observations, the group's observations, or from the individual himself.

In this exercise, the people identified as "it" stand and form a tight circle with interlocking arms. They may face either inward or outward depending on whether the person trying to break in sees them as simply involved with each other and ignoring him (face in), or as deliberately attempting to keep him out (face out). The outsider then tries to break through into the circle in whatever way he can, and the group members try to keep him out (Shultz, 1967. p. 131).

Again, after the exercise is allowed to continue for a period of time, the "it" is asked to share his feelings about himself and about the group. The group is also asked to share their feelings, and finally the entire group membership is asked to make observations. The group leader must insure that the physical effort in this exercise does not exceed a reasonable level, so that nobody will get physically hurt. This is of particular concern if the "it" person appears to be the "macho" man and seems to have the ability to be extremely competitive.

Elementary school teachers may recall this type of activity that was probably an accidental psychodrama technique call "Red Rover, Red Rover," in which children formed a line holding hands, and the child who was "it" had to attempt to break through the line to the other side. It is not recommended that the small group game become anywhere near as violent as the children's version often became.

A technique that was used by Dr. Cecil Osborn at seminars in order to get people in touch with their feelings rather quickly, might be criticized by some people, but those who have seen this technique all seem to agree that it can be very effective without any apparent danger to the participant or to any of the other people in the group.

A chair is placed in the middle of the group. A very heavy pad or cushion is placed on the chair. The participant is asked to kneel in front of the chair with eyes closed and begin to "pound" the cushion while repeating the word "No" or "Don't." The word really isn't important. What is important is the combination of the kinetic pounding and the repeating of the word. The client is encouraged to pound ever harder and call out the word louder. In most cases, the participant (if he really "gets into" the exercise) will change the word to another one, or to a phrase, and become more arid more in touch with feelings that may have been hidden to himself and to others who know him. After a reasonable period of time has passed (this should not be allowed to continue too long), the participant is asked to share certain feelings with the rest of the group.

The leader may ask questions like, "Who were you pounding?" "How did you feel while you were pounding?" "What did you learn from the experience?"

Some of the replies that may be heard are: "I suddenly realized how much I resented my father's efforts at controlling everything that I try to do." "I was aware of the amount of fear that I have of my boss (wife, mother-in law, girlfriend, boyfriend, etc.)." It is always wise to have the group give some positive input to the participant. Before going on to another activity, the leader may suggest that a few of the members share a group hug to reinforce the participant's acceptance by the members of the group.

I have used many of these techniques in marriage seminars or sensitivity seminars in churches with larger groups of people. Most of the techniques work well even with the larger group, but it is necessary at times to divide the entire group into smaller ones so that everyone can to be near enough to the action.

The reader is referred to Merle Ohlson's book, *Group Counseling*, 3rd edition, for many more effective techniques that can be used to stimulate feeling and discussion. The goal, of course, is not just to become aware of feelings that may have been repressed, but also to open the way for true healing and restoration (and deliverance) from the effects that those feelings and memories have had on the life of the individual.

USE THE SCORE ON ONE OF THE PERSONALITY INVENTORIES

This technique has already been discussed somewhat earlier in the book. The use of personality inventories or personality profiles opens the door for individual members of the group to begin disclosure as soon as possible without undue anxiety. The group facilitator should take the test himself so that he can lead the way in sharing his profile with the group as an example to help the others feel the freedom to share.

The group leader must become very familiar with the personality inventory of whatever test is to be used. He should be somewhat of an expert in the various items on the test and their significance. Most people taking a personality inventory such as the MMPI will experience considerable anxiety over the evaluations. They will need to be reassured that they are not seriously (or in most cases mildly) in trouble emotionally. There will be times when an individual will need to be told before the beginning of the sessions that he or she should seek personal counseling and not participate in the group. This needs to be done very tactfully so as not to create any more anxiety in the individual than is necessary.

When any of the subjective tests or inventories are used, it is necessary for the leader to inform the group members that the test is only as good as their willingness to be completely honest in answering the items. Occasionally, a group member will complain that the test was not accurate in its appraisal. At these times, the leader can note that the test only revealed what the person indicated in their answer to the items. It is possible that someone might misunderstand an item and thus answer it incorrectly, but a good test or inventory will have several items on each area of personality, so that even if one or two items are answered incorrectly, the overall evaluation will still be valid.

Yokefellows. Inc. located in Burlingame, California as part of the Burlingame Counseling Center, has many tests that can be purchased for use with special groups. In addition to the MMPI and the Draw a Person (DAP) test, the following are also available.

The use of any of the subjective tests listed in this text involves giving the members an opportunity to share their score and their reactions to the scores. The MMPI that is available from Yokefellows is scored by computer at the counseling center and the members are each sent an evaluation slip every two weeks. These slips convey to the person certain personality traits that were indicated by the test, with an evaluation by a trained psychometrist. There are suggestions on what the person can do to correct any problems, and there are readings, both in a text and in the Bible that can be helpful.

At each Yokefellow meeting, members are encouraged to share their slip and their feeling about what the slip says. Members of the group are encouraged to respond to the feelings and concerns of the member about his or her slip. There should never be any attempt to offer a diagnosis of any kind.

The Marriage Enrichment Inventory. This test is specifically designed for use by couples. It deals with twelve important areas of personality normally associated with success or failure in marriage. Among these are: Attitudes Toward the Opposite Sex; Dependency Feelings; Sexual Attitudes; Self-identity; Communication; Ability to Give and Receive Love; Attitudes Toward Money; plus five other important personality traits fundamental to a happy marriage relationship. There are several books listed in the Bibliography that can be used with this and each of the other tests listed here.

Human Relationships Test. This is a remarkable test, measuring the basic needs and responses in highly important areas, some of which are: Aggression, Dominance, Exhibition, Nurturance, etc. This test is helpful for everyone, but particularly effective for couples, helping them to better understand each other. A total of fifteen evaluation slips are sent, one every two weeks for thirty weeks. Books for use with this test are also listed in the Bibliography.

Self-Scoring Youth R Test. This is a test for young people, between the ages of twelve and twenty, designed to deal with six areas of particular importance to this age group: School, Acceptance By Peer Group, Relationship with Parents, Self-Acceptance, Boy-Girl relationships, and Sexual Attitudes.

Life Potential Inventory. This is a very comprehensive test covering eighteen highly significant areas of personality. A total of eighteen evaluation slips are sent to group members over a period of thirty-six weeks. There are four general classifications measuring: Aspects of Poise, Ascendance and Self-assurance; Socialization, Maturity and Responsibility; Achievement Potential, Intellectual Efficiency, Cooperative Action; and Emotional Tempo, Flexibility and Tender- mindedness.

OTHER USEFUL TESTING MATERIALS

The Self-Portrait Inventory: This test was developed by Oldham, J. and Morris, L. (1990) and can be found in their book, Personality Self-Portrait, *Why You Think, Work, Love, And/Act The Way You Do*. The book is published by Bantam Books in New York. The self-scoring test contains 104 items that the participant must answer Y (Yes, I agree), M (Maybe I agree), and N (No, I don't agree). The individual scores his or her own test and records the answers on a score sheet that is provided. The scores are then computed and placed on a graph that lists the following personality items:

Vigilant	Sensitive
Solitary	Devoted
Idiosyncratic	Conscientious
Adventurous	Leisurely
Mercurial	Aggressive
Dramatic	Self-Sacrificing
Self-Confident	

The text of the book goes into great detail in describing each of the thirteen areas. The reader will also learn about ways of dealing with areas that are of concern. The Self-Portrait is not intended to be used as a diagnostic tool but rather as an excellent means to self discovery. Caution: all of the tests that are mentioned in this book, as well as the many others referred to in the Bibliography, are what is known as subjective tests. The results are only as valid and reliable as the honesty of the answer recorded by the person taking the test. There can be considerable danger in permitting members of a group to think that there is something wrong with them or the tests. The test can only report what the individual puts down as an answer. Some of the tests, such as the MMPI or Millon's Personality Inventory are a little more reliable because the questions are well-constructed so that the person taking the test may not realize the significance of the question. Any interpretation, beyond the general inference of these tests, would of necessity, come from a psychometrist, one trained in the giving and assessing of tests.

DISC is a quadrant behavioral model based on the work of William Moulton Marston Ph.D. (1893–1947) to examine the behavior of individuals in their environment or within a specific situation (otherwise known as environment). It therefore focuses on the styles and preferences of such behavior. This system of dimensions of observable behavior has become known as the universal language of behavior. The research has found that characteristics of behavior can be grouped into these four major "personality styles" and they tend to exhibit specific characteristics common to that particular style. All individuals possess all four, but what differs from one to another is the extent of each. The assessments classify four aspects of behavior by testing a person's preferences in word associations (compare with Myers-Briggs Type Indicator). DISC is an acronym for:

- **D**ominance – relating to control, power and assertiveness
- **I**nfluence – relating to social situations and communication

- **S**teadiness (submission in Marston's time) – relating to patience, persistence, and thoughtfulness

- **C**onscientiousness (or caution, compliance in Marston's time) – relating to structure and organization

These four dimensions can be grouped in a grid with "D" and "I" sharing the top row and representing extroverted aspects of the personality, and "C" and "S" below representing introverted aspects. "D" and "C" then share the left column and represent task-focused aspects, and "I" and "S" share the right column and represent social aspects. In this matrix, the vertical dimension represents a factor of **"Assertive"** or **"Passive"**, while the horizontal represents **"Open"** vs. **"Guarded"**.

- **Dominance**: People who score high in the intensity of the "D" styles factor are very active in dealing with problems and challenges, while low "D" scores are people who want to do more research before committing to a decision. High "D" people are described as demanding, forceful, egocentric, strong willed, driving, determined, ambitious, aggressive, and pioneering. Low D scores describe those who are conservative, low keyed, cooperative, calculating, undemanding, cautious, mild, agreeable, modest and peaceful.

- **Influence:** People with high "I" scores influence others through talking and activity and tend to be emotional. They are described as convincing, magnetic, political, enthusiastic, persuasive, warm, demonstrative, trusting, and optimistic. Those with low "I" scores influence more by data and facts, and not with feelings. They are described as reflective, factual, calculating, skeptical, logical, suspicious, matter of fact, pessimistic, and critical.

- **Steadiness:** People with high "S" styles scores want a steady pace, security, and do not like sudden change. High "S" individuals are calm, relaxed, patient, possessive, predictable, deliberate, stable, consistent, and tend to be unemotional and poker faced. Low "S" intensity scores are those who like change and variety. People with low "S" scores are described as restless, demonstrative, impatient, eager, or even impulsive.

- **Conscientious:** People with high "C" styles adhere to rules, regulations, and structure. They like to do quality work and do it right the first time. High "C" people are careful, cautious, exacting, neat, systematic, diplomatic, accurate, and tactful. Those with low "C" scores challenge the rules and want independence and are described as self-willed, stubborn, opinionated, unsystematic, arbitrary, and unconcerned with details. (Wikipedia)

The Firo-B Test: The Firo-B (Fundamental Interpersonal Relations Orientation Behavior) questionnaire was developed by Will Schutz, Department of Psychiatry, Albert Einstein College of Medicine, Yeshiva University. The individual taking the test is instructed to answer in accordance to how they really are and not how they think they should be. The questionnaire measures temperament, not abnormal behavior. It also measures the expressive and responsive scores in all three areas of temperament needed, i.e. - inclusion, control, and affection. The questionnaire will indicate certain types of personality temperament such as: Melancholy, Choleric, Sanguine, Supine and Phlegmatic. As indicated earlier, it is not advisable when using this test instrument in groups to allow people to become preoccupied with the "tags" or labels. In no case should the group members be allowed to use their own "temperament label" as an excuse for their behavior.

Millon's Personality Inventory: the Millon personality profile tests various aspects of personality, arid although the test is intended for individual counseling measurement, the results of the test can also be a basis for group counseling, especially with individuals who may have some background in psychology. Millon (1981) lists the following eight personality styles: 1) Detached Passive; 2) Detached Active; 3) Dependent Passive; 4) Dependent Active; 5) Independent Passive; 6) Independent Active; 7) Ambivalent

Passive; and 8) Ambivalent Active. Although most people will show a higher score in one of the areas, everyone will have some score in all or almost all of the areas making it a possible tool for groups.

The use of any of the above mentioned tests, or any test for that matter, must not be considered an end in and of itself. The test or questionnaires are only to be used as tools to assist group members to get in touch with their feelings. The purpose of diagnosing personality problems is not the function of these tests. However, from time to time, a group leader may become aware of a group member with a problem that is beyond the scope of the group experience because of one of the tests (MMPI in particular) and feels it is prudent to suggest that the individual seek further individual help.

"You must look into other people as well as at them."

-Lord Chesterfield

CHAPTER 6:

SOME TECHNIQUES FOR GROUPS

The reader should already be aware that this author does not approve of using games or other activities just for the sake of "doing something." There are times when the leader or one of the group members may want to engage in some of the following activities because it seems that nothing is happening in the group. The group must learn that at times, "nothing" can be the beginning of a meaningful exchange. These activities in this chapter are intended to be used for specific purposes, and it is the leader's responsibility to see to it that they are not misused.

SENSITIVITY TRAINING

The leader may determine that the group needs some help with sensitivity awareness, or the group may have been formed with the express purpose of increasing sensitivity in interpersonal relationships. If this is the case one or more of the following Gestalt type activities may be employed:

Trust Awareness Training:

When the group needs to become aware of the importance of trust and their particular lack of trust, the leader can use the following technique:

1. The members are asked to form a circle (not too large). Each member, one at a time, is asked to stand in the middle of the circle and close his eyes. The person in the middle is told to stand with body stiff and fall over to the back or front and allow the people in the circle to hold him up. The people in the circle then hold the member up and pass him around the circle being careful not to let him fall. This exercise requires considerable trust by the person in the circle as he (or she) must trust the others to keep him

from falling as they pass him around. After a short time of passing the person around, the group stops, and the individual in the middle is asked to share how he or she felt during the exercise. Were there some times that there was a question in the persons mind as to whether someone in the group would not do his/her job? Knowing the people in the group, were there one or two that the middle person was concerned about?

2.   Another trust exercise involves the members breaking into couples. It is wise to make sure that people of fairly equal stature and weight are grouped together. Each couple is asked to take turns being "it." One person stands with his eyes closed while the other stands directly behind him. The person in front is told to simply fall in a stiff fashion backwards, while the other individual is to catch the faller. The individuals are then told to change places and repeat the exercise. After everyone has completed the exercise, the group should reconvene and share the feelings each had during the experience. Was it difficult relaxing completely into the hands of the catcher? Was there a temptation to reach back to break the fall? Did anyone feel tempted not to catch the person? What was learned about one's ability to trust?

3.   Trust Lift. In this exercise a number of people (at least five or six on each side) form a line on each side of a member who has been asked to lie in the floor on his or her back. The person who is "it" is told to remain stiff at all times with eyes closed. Without instructing the others the leader shows them what to do. Each member on either side is to place their hands under the one lying on the floor. When the leader nods his head, the rest gently lift the person into the air. They are shown by the leader how to lift and lower the subject and to sway to and fro. This exercise is very effective in teaching about trust. The subject must believe that the others can be trusted to not drop him or to cause him any harm.

4.   Blind Man's Walk. In this exercise the group is again divided into couples. One of the couple is blindfolded. The other member is told that he is to be the guide and lead the blindfolded subject around a predetermined obstacle course. The course should

include stairs, various obstacles, such as trees or posts, and overhangs that must be avoided. The blindfolded "blind man" must show complete trust in the guide. Trust may not necessarily be learned in one session of this exercise, but individuals will be able to discover the level of their trust. After every one in the group has had an opportunity to function in each of the roles, the group reconvenes and discusses their individual feelings during the exercise. "How did you feel while being led about without being able to see where you were going?" "How did you feel being totally responsible for the safely of your partner?" As the guide, did you feel that the blind person trusted you at all times? How did it feel to not be completely trusted? These and other questions may be used to stimulate discussion and personal disclosure regarding problems that members have experienced for most of their life. This in turn will offer an opportunity to seek the roots of the individual's ability to completely trust others.

5. Territoriality. In another chapter of this text, a mention was made of the research that was conducted with inmates in prison to determine territorial sensitivity. In the group activity, this technique can be used to help members become more aware of their level of tolerance or territoriality. The group is asked to sit in a circle within a few inches of each other with their eyes closed. They are then asked to put their arms straight up into the air above their heads. The leaders tell them to move their arms around and explore the space about them. They are encouraged to explore more and more of the space above their heads. During the exercise members are almost bound to touch someone else's hand. After a few minutes of this, the leader asked the group to share their experiences. "How did you feel when you touched someone else's hand, or they touched you?" Some of the members will express considerable agitation at having someone intrude into their space, while others will not have experienced any negative feelings about being touched. This is a good time to discuss together the concept of "touch and no touch" people. Touch people actually enjoy touching and being touched by others. No touch people are very uncomfortable with being touched. A no touch person will pull his

hand away if accidentally touched by someone else.

COMMUNICATION SKILLS

One of the causes of interrelational problems has to do with the inability to communicate successfully with others. The following exercises can help people understand more fully, the problems with communication and the importance of learning good communication skills. After each of the following exercises the group should be allowed to share their feelings about the exercise. After each exercise, the couples should tell each other what they were trying to say in each exercise.

1. The group is divided into couples (if the group is a married couples group it is advisable to have husbands and wives coupled together. First, the couple is to sit on the floor, back to back. All of the couples are told to try to communicate with each other at the same time without turning around or even to the side. The confusion of everyone talking at the same time will make communication almost impossible and even frustrating. Next the couple is told to face each other and close their eyes. They are then told to try to communicate by touching each other's face with their fingers, taking turns talking with their fingers while the other member has their eyes closed. The couples are then told to open their eyes and try to communicate with each other with their eyes only. Again after each has had a turn at trying to communicate, they are asked to share what it was that they were trying to say with their eyes.

After all of the above exercises are completed, the entire group should share their feelings of frustration and insights their need for learning better communication skills. This type of activity will often develop into discussions between married couples about some of their problems of communicating with each other. It can be the beginning of healing and restoration. Psychologists say that one of the biggest causes of problems among married couples is a failure to communicate effectively.

ROLE PLAYING

Role playing can be an effective way of learning to see things through the eyes of someone else. Asking a member of the group to play the role of a child to another member's role as parent will often result in the parent member discovering feelings about childhood or their parents that they had successfully repressed in the past. These feelings need to be dealt with in the present, once the member is aware of his/her childhood feelings; it is possible for the group to help the member work through these problems. Other role play activities include:

- Ask a member to "play" the role of his father or mother with another member who plays the teenager.

- Have a member play the role of his or her boss.

- Many other role playing activities will come out as a result of the interaction of the group.

Role play is to be thought of as a confrontation technique. An alert leader will find many situations in which the technique can be used. It is less threatening to attack, or be attacked, while in a role than when being oneself. "The insights gained through skillful use of this confrontation technique usually are most satisfactory," according to Bates and Johnson (1975). The technique of role play includes the Role Reversal technique. In this activity, a member is asked to play a role of someone else. The leader, or another member, may play the antagonist to the person in role reversal. This is a psychodramatic technique in which the person "becomes" a significant other or a part of himself. Role reversal may be used with married couples. The couple is asked to reverse roles, so that the husband becomes the wife and the wife becomes the husband. They then act out a situation that has, in the past, caused them problems. This is a good way to gain insight into how the other person may feel about a given situation. It is important that the person(s) involved in the role play or role reversal assume as many of the perceived characteristics of the role they are playing as possible, They should assume the posture, body language, tone of voice, etc., so that as true a portrayal as possible is accomplished.

The rest of the members of the group are asked to respond at the end of the role play session after the two members have had an opportunity to respond to each other.

HUMAN POTENTIAL (OTTO, 1970)

The Human Potential Seminar is based on the assumption that: *"Something is right with an individual instead something being wrong."* The first step is to have a member tell the rest of the group all of the things that he or she thinks are their personal strengths. Next the group will offer a "Strength Bombardment" by telling the member what strengths they see in him or her. The member asks, "What do you see that is preventing me from using my strengths?" Again the group responds. The next step consists of the group developing a fantasy of what the target person can be doing in five years or more if he or she used their strengths. As a final step, the target member is asked to share with the group how he or she felt in undergoing this experience.

According to Otto, a second portion of this seminar is the "Success Bombardment" in which the subject begins telling the group about the most successful experiences of his entire life, followed by two or three unsuccessful experiences. The group is asked to analyze the unsuccessful experiences in the light of the successful ones and in so doing help the subject through the "Success Bombardment" to see whether the failures represented the non-application of his success typical pattern and to suggest areas where he has not tapped his full potential.

A third section of the HPS focuses on action and consists of goal setting experiences. According to Otto, at the close of each session, members of the group set individual goals which are to be accomplished before the next session, or at the end of two or three sessions. The goals must be: 1) capable of being put into words, 2) believable, 3) measurable, 4) something the members really want to do, and 5) presented with no alternatives. Bates and Johnson (1975) conclude that, "the purpose of this procedure is to help members become aware that they can control their own lives to a far greater degree than they probably do at the present time." It also helps members to become aware of their own value systems and increases self-motivation.

SOCIOGRAM: INTERACTION DIAGRAM

In this exercise the members are asked to diagram, with arrows, the interaction of a given period of time of group discussion. This calls attention to the cross-currents within a group. Who did most of the talking? To whom was most of the discussion directed? Who did not participate in the discussion at all? What was the degree of eye contact during the interchanges?

CHILDHOOD MEMORIES

In this exercise the members are asked to recall some of their earliest memories. Members are then asked to share those memories with the group. What was the significance of the memory? Who was involved in the memory? In what way were they involved?

At times this exercise can be a little more structured. The members are asked to think about their home at the time they were very young (some people will remember as far back as their very early childhood, others will not be able to go as far back). They are to spend some time visiting the home in which they lived, trying to see all of the people who would have been there at the time. Sometime using soft music in the background while this exercise is being conducted will help the members to focus. After a period of time, the members are asked to share their experiences and the feeling that those experiences evoked. Others in the group are asked to act as reflectors and share with the person what they hear them saying. It is important that the leader or the other members refrain from trying to analyze the meaning of any of the experiences for the sharing member.

Bates and Johnson (1975) list many other techniques that can be used to help create a confrontation that will lead to the kind of interchange among members that result in self-disclosure. Some of the techniques will produce mild confrontation, while others will produce moderate to strong confrontation. The object of confrontation techniques is to have the confrontation in the safe, loving atmosphere of the group with a leader in charge who will be able to prevent unwanted reactions. Some of the other techniques listed by Bates and Johnson are:

Free Association	Taking a Trip
Druthers	Presentation of Self: Clothing
Symbolic Substitution	Drifting
New Names	Magic Shop
Best Possible Way of Life	Identifying Emotions
Stereotyping	And many others.

MICRO-LAB

The micro lab is also found in Bates and Johnson. It is presented here in an abbreviated form to show the general use of the technique. The entire group is divided into two groups —A and B. The A group is asked to sit in a small circle facing each other. The B group sits or stands behind them as observers. Each member of the A group will have a "feedback" partner in the B group. After the A group has met for seven minutes in discussion, they will each meet with their feedback partner for feedback on his or her behavior during the seven minutes. After the feedback session, the B group will meet for seven minutes in discussion as did the A group. After seven minutes the B group will meet with their respective A group "feedback partner" for feedback on their behavior. Before the meeting begins, a timekeeper should be appointed to keep the sessions on schedule.

Bates and Johnson (1975) in Chapter 8 list some of the nonverbal confrontation techniques. The use of these techniques requires some instruction by the leader regarding non-verbal communication (see Chapter 4 of this text). After the group has been instructed about these non-verbal signs, they are asked to make notes of any of the indications of non-verbal communication.

BODY LANGUAGE

The group should be aware of the messages that are being transmitted by the body language of other members of the group. Some of the things to watch for are:

HANDS AND FEET

The tightly closed fist or the thumb tightly enclosed in the fist suggesting to group leaders and group members to proceed with caution. When both thumbs are tightly enclosed in the fist it should serve as a "red-flag" to the entire group. The twirling of a ring, the cracking of knuckles, and the intertwining of fingers all carry different non-verbal messages that can greatly enhance the effectiveness of the group. Feet stretched out into the group is probably sending a different message than feet tucked up under the body, or under a chair. A person with arms folded over the chest is saying, "I am not receiving what you are saying" or "I dare you to convince me!"

Facial expressions transmit many signals. It is estimated that over 55 percent of the meaning of what is being said can be interpreted from facial expressions. Eye contact, or the absence of eye contact, sends two different messages. For more on this see Chapter 3 on "Group Dynamics."

Another technique for stimulating discussion, or to increase sensitivity among the group members, involves the use of the tape recorder or the video camera. The session may be recorded on tape (with the permission of the group) to be listened to at the next session. The group is asked to respond by evaluating the group's discussion. The leader may need to edit the tape down to a few examples for the sake of time.

Use of a video camera is also an excellent way to evaluate body language. Showing the film without the sound track can help members begin to see the effects of certain non-verbal forms of communication. Here again, the leader may need to edit the tape to fit into a reasonable time period. The reader is reminded of the personal example offered by this author of the doctoral project in which doctoral students were asked to view parts of the video that had been made of the entire weekend session of a Marathon Group held at San Diego State University.

All of the techniques suggested here and in the work by Bates and Johnson can help stimulate interaction between the members of the group, bringing about greater sensitivity to one's own feelings, the feelings of others, and evoke confrontation on a mild, moderate or more severe level. The leader of the group must be able to decide when an activity is necessary and be able to predetermine the goals of each activity. Some caution must be used in the use of any of the psychodrama techniques, because there is always a possibility of evoking feelings and reactions that can be threatening to the rest of the group. Even when the leader has taken every precaution in omitting borderline personalities from the group, occasionally one will slip through.

In one group held at the Burlingame Counseling Center many years ago, during a highly emotional interchange between members, one lady jumped to her feet and ran from the room and the building into the night screaming hysterically. She was later picked up by the police and taken to the psychiatric ward of a local hospital. The incident, although slightly embarrassing to the staff at the counseling center, was not too serious. The lady was released in a few days, but was not allowed to return to the group. She needed the controlled attention of an individual counseling session.

There are other techniques available to the leader that can be used. However, many of them require special training and even a degree in testing and test interpretation. These techniques should only be used in a controlled institutional setting such as a hospital with the presence of a trained therapist who could assist in case of unexpected difficulties.

"He that is thy friend indeed, He will help thee in thy need If thou sorrow, he will weep If thou wake, he cannot sleep Thus of every grief in heart He with thee does bear a part. These are certain signs to know Faithful friend from flattering foe."

- WILLIAM SHAKESPEARE

CHAPTER 7:

TWELVE STEP PROGRAM

Over the past many years, I (Dr. DeKoven) have been conducting workshops and seminars across the country and internationally. The results have been most gratifying as believers begin to fully grasp God's overall plan for the healing and restoration of their lives. For many, the awareness of the Lord's great love, graciousness and power to transform lives, has had a liberating affect for which He deserves all the glory!

One of the needs expressed by many has been to have an ongoing group for those struggling to become whole in Christ. In praying about this need, I have chosen to adopt the Twelve Step model of Alcoholics Anonymous as a guide, with certain modifications that beautifully corresponds to the three stages of our spiritual development as described in my book, *Journey to Wholeness.*

This book is to be used in small group formats, as you will see in the "Group Process" section. It is my hope that many will find complete healing and wholeness regardless of the level of dysfunction of the family they were raised in, for God can save us to the uttermost and transform even the chief of all sinners into the glorious image of His Son. This book can be used in various recovery formats to include grief and loss, adult children of alcoholics, etc.

There is really no special magic or unique key to resolving past conflict and achieving peace in the inner man. It is a process that requires diligent hard work, discipline and patience to trust the Lord and the process. These characteristics are not normally part of one who was raised in a dysfunctional family. In fact, if you were able to easily discipline yourself to apply scripture to your life, you wouldn't need this book! So be aware! All of us using this program are fellow strugglers, *"Working out our own salvation with fear and trembling,"* (see Philippians 2:12).

Before beginning this, or any other *Twelve Step* study group process, it is important to ask yourself some important questions. Your answers will help you determine your readiness for the group process and very possibly your future success.

1. Can you commit yourself to the time involved?

[ ] Yes   [ ] No

Ideally the group should be a high priority. I recommend that you develop and participate in a 13 to 25 week program, meeting weekly for 2 hours. This is in addition to your other church related obligations. Make sure that barring an emergency, you can complete your commitment to yourself, the group and the Lord. If you are unsure, seek counsel from your spiritual leadership, especially your pastor.

2. Do you really want to change?

[ ] Yes   [ ] No

Many people will start a group hoping that their spouse will change; their circumstances will change, etc. We must accept the reality that the only person we can change is ourselves, with God's help and power. This group is designed for you to focus in on making changes in your life, transforming your mind, circumcising your heart. Be willing to trust the process. You did not develop physically overnight and you will not change emotionally and spiritually overnight. We must trust in the Lord to fully guide us. (See Proverbs 3:5-6).

3. Are you willing to submit to the process of change?

[ ] Yes   [ ] No

Jesus said that if you are to build a house, you must first *"count the cost…"* Growing in the Lord comes through discipline (see Hebrews 12) or teaching. This is not a painless process. As you go through the steps, you may feel worse before you feel better. This is expected. Again, you must be certain that you will complete the program before you begin. Once you have determined that you can and will make your best effort to allow the Lord to minister to you through the *Twelve Step* process, you are ready to take the next step.

4. Read

Most people find it helpful to read my books, *Journey to Wholeness*, or *Grief Relief* for grief and loss recovery as a prerequisite to beginning the group. Further, listening to the teaching tapes based on these books can be of assistance in understanding the general plan that God has for us. It is recommended that you read beforehand, but if you cannot do so, the reading can be completed during the first three weeks of the group. You will find in *Journey to Wholeness* a typology of our physical/emotional development to maturity and our spiritual growth process. This gives you the "big picture" of God's marvelous plan. There is very little in this book that can be claimed as "new." It is a synthesis of the plan of God for our lives, presented in an understandable format. Neither this book, nor any other, is a substitute for the personal study of God's Word. Remember to read the Word of God daily along with doing your questions in this book, as you take your first steps toward transformation. *Grief Relief* was written for those who have suffered a significant loss. If you are in a grief process, the group and *Grief Relief* will help. It lists the specific stages of grief, the process of mourning and the hope that we have in Jesus Christ.

5. We have a head start.

It is important to remember that we have many things going for us as Christians, because of what Jesus has done for us through His atonement on the cross. These include:

a. When He ascended to be with His Father, "He led captivity captive," (Ephesians 4:8). That is, all that binds, wounds, hurts, and destroys us was ultimately broken and eradicated for time and eternity on the cross of Calvary. All the guilt and shame, every dysfunctional thought and painful feeling was borne for us on the cross. We rely on the blood of Jesus, His power and sufficiency to continue to cleanse and restore us.

b. "Therefore He is also able to save forever those who draw near to God through Him, since He always lives to make intercession for them," (Hebrews 7:25). What a wonderful thought to know that we have such a powerful advocate. Jesus is now interceding (pleading our case and defending us) for us to His Father in heaven.

c. Jesus has given the Holy Spirit, Comforter (John 14 through 16), and Counselor to us. He comes along side of us, assisting us in our walk. He also reveals truth and will lovingly bring to the surface anything in our lives that needs transformation by God's great power. As we yield ourselves to Him, He will remove every stain, spot, or wrinkle from our lives, and prepare us to be His glorious bride (Ephesians 5:27). This is now happening throughout the Body of Christ, and this guide is one of many tools to be used for this purpose.

d. Christ gave to the church the five-fold ministry to teach, train, exhort, rebuke, correct and encourage (Ephesians 4:11-12) His children to come to a place of completeness in Christ, conformed to His image. With all of these and the deposit of the gifts and grace in each of us, we can rest assured that in due time, we will become all God created us to be.

THE PROBLEM

Perhaps some of the following characteristics describe you as they do many adult children of dysfunctional families or those who have experienced a significant loss. I have outlined them for you here. Open your heart and mind to the Holy Spirit's work in your life, but remember, "There is no condemnation to those in Christ Jesus," (Romans 8:1).

1. We become isolated and afraid of people and authority figures. Angry people and personal criticism frighten us. We either become dysfunctional ourselves or marry someone who is or both.

We find a compulsive personality, such as a workaholic, to fulfill our subconscious need for abandonment.

2. We view life as victims, and we are attracted to weakness in our love, friendship and career relationships.

3. We have an overdeveloped sense of responsibility and it is easy for us to be concerned with others rather than ourselves. This helps us to avoid looking too closely at our own faults and to avoid responsibility for ourselves. Somehow we feel guilty if we stand up for ourselves instead of giving in to others.

4. We become addicted to excitement in all our affairs, we confuse love with pity and we tend to rescue others and try to "fix" them.

5. We have denied feelings from our traumatic childhood and have lost the ability to express even comfortable feelings such as joy or happiness.

6. We judge others harshly and fear the judgment of others; yet we also criticize and judge others.

7. We are terrified of abandonment and will do almost anything to hold onto a relationship rather than experience the painful feeling of abandonment. We develop this from living in a compulsive environment where no one was emotionally "there" for us.

8. As all compulsions are a part of a family dysfunction, we took on symptoms early in childhood and carried them into adulthood. Even though we may never act out compulsive behavior ourselves, we have acquired unhealthy behavior patterns that have given us difficulty, especially in our intimate relationships.

This is a description, not an indictment. We have learned to survive by becoming reactors, rather than actors. We have learned that we can unlearn, however, as described in "The Solution."

Further, there are many rules we have learned in our dysfunctional family environment. These rules can bind us in our present life circumstances. Some of the rules are described here.

RULES LEARNED BY CHILDREN IN SHAME-BASED FAMILIES

Each family has rules. There are rules about celebrating and socializing, rules about touching and sexuality; rules about sickness and proper health care; rules about vacations and vocations; rules about household maintenance and spending money. Perhaps the most important rules are about feelings, interpersonal communication and parenting.

Toxic shame (shame of oneself that poisons a person's thinking, feeling and behavior) is consciously transferred through shaming rules which are passed down through each generation. Some of these are:

> **Control**: One must be in control of all feelings, interactions and personal behavior at all times.
>
> **Perfection**: Always be right in everything you do. We learn to live according to an external image, an imposed measurement to which no one measures up.
>
> **Blame**: Whenever things don't turn out as planned, blame yourself or others.
>
> **Denial of the Five Freedoms**: Don't perceive, think, feel, desire, or imagine the ways you do; do these the way the perfectionist ideal demands.
>
> **The No-talk Rule**: Don't speak of your loneliness and sense of self-rapture.
>
> **Don't Make Mistakes**: Mistakes reveal the flawed, vulnerable self. To acknowledge a mistake is to open yourself up to scrutiny. Cover up your own mistakes and if someone else makes one, shame them.

Unreliability: Don't expect reliability in relationships. Don't trust anyone, and you will never be disappointed.

GRIEF RESPONSE

When a person suffers a significant loss, whether through divorce, death, or the loss of a friend or job, the reactions can be enormous. Although everyone responds differently to loss, based on past experiences and individual differences, it is universally painful. There are certain stages of grief that have been identified by behavioral scientists and must be processed for emotional, psychological and spiritual health and recovery. For the majority of men and women raised in dysfunctional families, a loss of the inner child or of childhood experiences occur, necessitating the development of denial and other defense mechanisms such as repression. When pain of loss, even loss in childhood is not resolved, a person can become "stuck" in their emotional growth. Therefore, a grief process is necessary for most people, whether due to adult losses or dysfunctional family life. To better understand the grief process the significant stages of grief are provided here. For more detailed information read, *Grief Relief.*

THE STAGES OF GRIEF

STAGE ONE: SHOCK

The first stage in grief is shock. With shock, a kind of numbness envelopes you.

Shock is nature's natural insulation, cushioning the severity of the blow. Shock is a physical experience in which you might feel odd physical sensations, a "spaced-out" feeling, and a tight knot in your stomach, or even the loss of your normal appetite.

You may notice that you become distressed over little things which normally would not mean that much to you, such as throwing a major tantrum when you discover a minor problem — perhaps it is the missing button on a favorite piece of clothing, or the failure of a child to take out the garbage — little things, made almost intolerable from the sudden shock of loss.

Or, you may not be able to remember small, common things such as your own phone number, or the name of a friend you see almost every day. These "memory blocks" are also a normal part of the shock stage.

Nervous laughter also occurs during this first stage of grief.

When I first heard that I had not been accepted into the college of my choice, my initial reaction was the inappropriate laughter of disbelief (a form of shock). I experienced shock in a similar way when my step-grandfather passed away. He was very special to me, and I didn't want to believe he was gone, and strange as it might seem, an almost uncontrollable laughter was the result.

Shock and numbness will not prevent you from doing what you must do. You will act, at least in part, instinctively. Whatever your situation, you will normally retain the capacity to be rational. The numbness will soon wear away and real grieving will begin.

Even without these particular symptoms of shock, you still may cry out from your heart something like this: "Oh no, I can't believe he or she is gone!"

This too, is a form of shock.

In some cases, a person may act as if their loved one had not died for hours (normal) or even days (not so normal — if it continues, seek help), or they will act as though the loss had not occurred at all.

When you are hurting, you may appear not to care about others, but you are relying on automatic behavior, without thinking, because you are in a state of shock.

During this stage you may say, "I don't know what's happening to me," or, "Why can't I do something. Why can't I think this through?" or even "Why don't I care about others?"

All of these reactions are normal for the first stage of grief — shock.

In time, the shock will wear off and you will once again come in contact with your real emotions.

STAGE TWO: DENIAL

Usually the stage after shock is denial.

Of course you understand intellectually what has happened through your loss, but on a deeper level, all of your habits and memories are denying the death or the loss that has occurred.

You may find yourself setting the wrong number of plates at the table or saving bits of news for someone who will never be able to hear them again.

In one case, when a man lost his job, he kept working at home on a major business report for his previous employer that he "just had to finish," even though he was no longer employed. It was only after his wife loudly confronted him, claiming he had to stop the denial behavior, that he finally broke down and cried, sobbing, "Why me? Why me?"

Denial may surface in some form or another for many months or years. There is no set time schedule for moving through this stage.

Some deny death or loss by staying away from the grave or other reminders of their lost loved one. Others leave the deceased's room unchanged for a period of time, but perhaps the most common type of denial is to just change the subject whenever circumstances about the pain or loss come up.

How many times, when you've questioned a friend or a relative about a shocking loss — such as a divorce — have you heard the answer, "I don't want to talk about it!?"

This is a normal denial and will usually subside after the pain subsides.

Do what feels proper for you as you move toward acceptance.

There is no absolute right or wrong time frames in these matters.

Please understand that keeping a few treasures and pictures in view indefinitely is not denial but simply an affirmation and a reminder of the love you shared. A part of you will always grieve, but soon, you will be able to accept the death of the one you love through the love of Jesus Christ Who strengthens you.

STAGE THREE: FANTASY vs. REALITY

The third stage of your transition is a struggle between fantasy and reality (this can actually be seen as a component of denial).

You may find yourself experiencing some of these fairly typical reactions that I have had voiced from my clients:

"When I get up and go to the kitchen for breakfast, I almost expect my spouse to be there, waiting to greet me with a morning kiss."

"I caught myself looking around the backyard expecting to see my child out there playing. I even brought my child's bike in from the rain so it wouldn't rust."

"I heard someone pull into the driveway, and for a moment I thought my sweetheart was home from grocery shopping."

"I saw her walking in the supermarket, and from the back I was sure it was my wife. I found myself walking faster to catch up to her, only to remember my wife was dead."

Perhaps you find yourself doing, or wanting to do the things the two of you have always done, such as getting the mail, going for walks, or paying bills together. These are short fantasies and are a very normal way of wishing that things were different, wishing that your loved one was still with you.

Whether you only think of these fantasies or act them out, consider them as transitory — they will pass. They are healthy ways of experiencing grief relief and only reflect the cry in your heart that you "wish they had not gone."

To want everything to be the same in your life —just as it was before the loss or death — is very normal!

Most people in the grief process frequently move in and out of these experiences, from fantasy to reality to fantasy, with little or no control over such movement.

Although this is frustrating and confusing at times, please do not be alarmed by the behavior. It is a very normal part of the process.

STAGE FOUR: GRIEF RELEASE

Sooner or later you will come to realize that your loss is real, and the pain of this reality will penetrate to your deepest self. You will cry and weep from deep within your gut. Your feelings will come pouring out like a fountain of sorrow. You may even feel as though you are losing control of your feelings and emotions. But do not let this worry you!

Since you first learned of your tremendous loss, you have come through many stages. These stages may have taken hours, days, or weeks, but you have come a long way! All the normal emotions that have been denied through these first stages now express themselves. It is a grief release.

Let it flow!

Let your emotions out!

This is one of God's ways of cleansing you from the pain.

After this grief release, much of your physical and emotional pain will fade away. Certainly the most noticeable and obvious signs of grief, such as shortness of breath, nausea, or choking sensations, will disappear.

Beware of those who try to comfort you by saying, "Don't cry, you'll be all right," or "Don't worry, God will take care of you."

These comments are well-intentioned, but are from misguided givers of advice just like Job's friends.

Do not hold back on your crying.

Do not try to tell yourself you are a "bad Christian" because you are not rejoicing that your loved one is with God.

Do not allow the devil to condemn you for a "loss of faith" because you are hurting; and those around you are saying, "Trust God, trust God."

The grief you are experiencing is God's way of releasing your emotions and pain!

You need the time to cry and release your feelings!

Yes, God has promised to take care of you, and one way He does this is by allowing your grief to be eased through crying and by getting your feelings out so that you are free of them.

If you severely cut your arm and the pain caused you to cry, not one of these same people would say to you, "Trust God, trust God." They'd tell you to cry, to let it out, because it hurts so much.

The same is true with grief. Emotional pain is no less real than the physical pain that comes with a cut arm!

You will always have the memories of the loss, but as with a scar from a wound long since healed, you will eventually no longer feel the sharp pain.

Do not reject those who try to give you false comfort. They are doing the only thing they know how to do to make you feel better. Just know that there is good health in releasing your feelings and easing your grief and that this process in no way indicates a lack of faith or lack of trust in God.

It is actually harmful to hold these emotions inside!

A grieving person, who keeps his feelings inside and delays their release for an extended period, may experience some strong negative reactions. These reactions can manifest themselves in physical problems such as ulcers, severe headaches, and other stress-related illnesses.

STAGE FIVE: LIVING WITH THE MEMORIES

After you have experienced the therapeutic flood of grief from the previous stage, the pain of grief begins to ease. You are now emerging from the process to the victory of GRIEF RELIEF.

However, grief's slow work is not yet finished.

When you go to church for the first time without your mate, you may feel the sharp pain of grief because of his or her absence from the pew beside you.

If a parent who has lived with you has died, you may be reminded of your loss when you receive a Christmas card addressed to them.

When you drive by the building where you used to work before you were fired, pangs of anxiety and inadequacy might envelop you.

In ALL these instances, you feel the hurt or grief again.

Naturally, on the first anniversary of the death of your loved one, you will be reminded of them and grieve. Naturally, when you meet an old work associate, who reminds you of the job you used to have, you will grieve.

These experiences are very real and a completely normal part of the grief relief process.

Learning to live with memories is a long-term task. You will meet people, go places and see things that remind you of your significant loss. In this stage, however, grief is not a constant painful process but is aroused by specific incidents that trigger old memories.

STAGE SIX: ACCEPTANCE; AFFIRMATION

In this stage, you are now beginning to accept the loss and to affirm in your own life that you will go on living.

Good memories of the deceased are brought to your mind without stabbing pain and often with gratitude and pleasure for such recollections.

If you've just lost a major job, after a period of mourning, there comes a time when you say, "That's it! I've got to get on with my life!"

When you are finally ready to decide to make a statement of acceptance such as ("I can't change it. It has happened, and it is over"), and a statement of affirmation ("It is time for me to start dating again") then you are well on your way to a healthy, normal life!

I encourage you to entertain good memories. Good memories will make it easier and easier to talk about your loved one and to appreciate your past relationship without wishing unrealistically that it could be restored.

You will start to show a renewed trust in yourself, as if to say, "I can make it." No matter how you express it, there is great hope when you begin to see good possibilities for yourself and your future.

Remember, often the process of grief relief takes years to fully complete.

There is no need to hurry it.

Grief moves at its own pace.

Trust the Holy Spirit; dedicate your grief process to the will of God and trust He will do a good work in you.

"For I am confident of this very thing, that He who began a good work in you will perfect it until the day of Christ Jesus." (Philippians 1:6).

During this stage of affirmation and acceptance, you will begin doing more things with others.

You may take your children to the beach and enjoy it. You may sponsor a wedding shower and not feel lonely for your deceased or ex-spouse.

You may go bowling with some of your ex-work associates without any strong pangs of remorse that you are no longer employed with their company.

You may reminisce about the good times you had with your spouse, and even laugh about some of the funny times but without the hurt.

You are finding new meaning in what you do.

Celebrate the memories of your deceased loved one without being obsessed by these memories!

Celebrate the positive parts of your old job, your ex-spouse (in a divorce) without being obsessed by the negative factors in these events!

"O give thanks to the LORD, for *He is* good; For His loving kindness is everlasting." (I Chronicles 16:34).

As mentioned above, it is possible and often the case, that one can become stuck or partially fixated in a stage of grief or normal growth. When this occurs, many symptoms can develop which limit the range of experience of an individual's life. This limitation, or dis-ease, is what primarily leads one into treatment. All of us desperately desire freedom, a sense of purpose and to follow the plans of God for our lives. If we become "stuck" in our growth process, we must work through the barriers that develop. That is the purpose of the recovery/restoration process.

HOW CAN I BE SURE I NEED THIS GROUP?

Over the past few years, especially through research done with alcoholics and drug abusers, a fairly comprehensive profile of personality traits and behavioral repertoire has been discovered that, when in combination, indicate the probability of an individual being raised in a dysfunctional family. The following is a checklist of symptoms. If you answer yes to 50% of these, you could probably benefit from a Twelve Step program. I would encourage you to answer each question and discover for yourself the need (if you have one, if not rejoice and help others) in your life.

BECOMING STUCK

For those in grief recovery, whether through being raised in a dysfunctional family or from significant loss, support is always helpful. If a person becomes unable to face their loss or process through to acceptance (in a reasonable time frame), a recovery group will be of significant benefit.

In the check list that follows, see if you identify yourself in several of the following traits. If you do, it's likely that you are co-dependent and are carrying your family dysfunction or are stuck in the grief relief process.

- Abandonment Issues — You fear that people you care for will leave you.

- Delusion and Denial —You are not facing the truth in real life situations.

- Undifferentiated ego mass —You lack independent thinking. You can't express yourself.

- Loneliness and Isolation (Self-explanatory)

- Thought disorders —You see hallucinations (seeing things not there) and hear voices.

- Control madness —You compulsively try to control everything, fear when not.

- Hyper-vigilant and high level anxiety —Perfectionism.

- Internalized shame — Self-loathing, not because you did badly, but because you ARE bad!

- Lack of boundaries — You let others violate you. You are unable to keep from victimization.

- Disabled will — You are unable to make healthy decisions.

- Reactive and reenacting — You react to others and repeat

the same old patterns.

- Equifinality —You are fatalistic, "What will be, will be."

- Numbed out — You have no sense of feeling at all.

- Offender with or without offender status — You have a sense of always wrong.

- Fixated personality — You are stuck acting in the same old way.

- Dissociated responses —There is a sense of you "not being here" when responding. You're out of touch.

- Yearning — Desire for parental warmth and approval.

- Secrets — Especially family secrets you can't tell.

- Faulty communication style — Placate, blame, project.

- Under involved —You withdraw from life.

- Neglect of development dependency needs — You don't nurture yourself. You have a poor self-image.

- Compulsive/Addictive — Same thing, without satisfaction.

- Trance — You carry the family spell.

- Intimacy problems — You can't get close or stay close to people.

- Over involved —You try to do everything to fill void.

- Narcissistically deprived — You never had anyone there just for you.

- Abuse victim — Physical, emotional, sexual.

- Lack of coping skills (under learning) — You are unable to do certain things. You did not learn.

- False self (confused identity) — You try to be what others expect, but not real self.

- Avoid depression — You fill in with many activities.

- Measured, judgmental and perfectionist — You have to, should have, must, ought, can't inhibited trust, but can't believe others could or would care.

- Loss of your own reality — You are so involved in pleasing others, you can't care for yourself.

- Inveterate dreamer —You are so heavenly minded, you are no earthly good!

- Emotional constraint — You lack the ability to express your feelings.

- Spiritual bankruptcy —You can't relate to God and His work in your life.

Again, if you said "yes" to 50% or more of these items, you probably suffer from dis-ease rooted in childhood dysfunction or significant loss, however, do not despair. As Christians, we have a hope in God and by the power of the Holy Spirit and the assistance of skilled helpers in the Body of Christ, healing and restoration is available.

THE SOLUTION

Though our parents gave us our physical existence, we now look to God, our Heavenly Father, as the initiator of our new life. We look to Him for direction to a new level of experience, a life of wholeness and healing of the past. We learn that we do not have to remain prisoners of our past.

Recovery begins when we learn about the problems of our family upbringing. We learn that it is three-fold: physical, spiritual and mental. We learn the three C's: we didn't cause it, we can't control it and we can't cure it. By educating ourselves about the problem, we begin a process that eventually leads us to forgiveness of our parents and the willingness to release them to God. We learn that real love cannot exist without the dimension of justice.

We learn to experience our feelings and then to express them. This builds self-esteem, which is a missing ingredient in our personalities. We learn that, in Christ, we are OK. We are not "crazy." With God's help and twelve steps based on scripture, we can recover from the effects of our traumatic loss or our negative family learning and turn our lives in a new and beautiful direction. As we learn to admit our powerlessness to change ourselves and other people, places and things, we let God begin to heal our thinking and our defects one day at a time. We learn to let God and the group nurture us, and we learn to nurture and accept ourselves and others. This also works effectively with the losses in our life, and we can overcome and renew our zest for living again.

As we begin to discover and love ourselves as God loves us, we will see beautiful changes in all our relationships — especially with our parents, ourselves and God. If we are married and if we have children, we will find healthier ways of interacting with these loved ones too. Finally, we become actors, rather than reactors. We will learn to risk new relationships without fear of rejection.

THE GROUP PROCESS

Small groups meeting together for a common purpose are not a new phenomenon (in spite of what many humanistic psychologists would teach). In fact, our present popular Home Group or Fellowship boom is a variation on a New Testament model (see Acts 2). Small groups and group process is a powerful forum whereby God can move on our behalf.

In small groups, as in any gathering of people, there must be certain rules and their agreed upon adherents. These must be strictly followed if positive results are to occur. Without some clear understanding, any group can degenerate into a dysfunctional pseudo-family that will repeat the patterns that caused the initial problems. Therefore, it is important that each group member read and acknowledge the following rules and to the best of their ability, follow them. (A copy of these rules and a place for voluntary signature is provided in the back of this book.)

GUIDELINES

1. Confidentiality/Anonymity -Each person in the group must have a sense that their basic boundaries will not be violated. One such guarantee of that is the pledge to allow all members of the group to have anonymity and confidentiality. All business transacted in the group is owned jointly by the group. As children raised in dysfunctional families, our right of privacy or even our thoughts and feelings was violated. It was not safe for us to share our feelings without reprisal. To assure confidentiality, we ask you to keep everything you hear confidential in our meetings. No member of this group is ever to be discussed outside of this group, not even with another group member We feel our healing is dependent upon the trust that we have in God and in one another and the freedom that we feel to share openly and honestly without fear of exposure outside of the meetings.

a. Therefore, we agree to keep all communication and identities anonymous and confidential.

2. Freedom to express feelings without judgment - As mentioned above, the freedom to express the full range of our emotions as children was controlled or criticized by our care givers. In the group, everyone must have the opportunity to express themselves without being put down. We do not need to be the Holy Spirit for others. In grief recovery, we need permission to express our feelings without condemnation.

a. Denial of Negative Emotions - It is very important that each member of this group feels free to express negative emotions such as pain, grief, or anger. Much compulsive behavior is the result of not being in touch with one's feelings or being afraid to acknowledge or express these feelings. We should never cut another person off with a statement such as, "You're forgetting the Lord can bring good out of this," or "You have to have faith that this will work out." Such statements are true, but they are not helpful when used to cut a person off from expressing feelings. If anything, they create more distress by their implication that the person suffering is lacking in faith and is somehow not a good Christian. When our feelings are discounted, we feel invalidated. We stop sharing our feelings and we lose hope of working through and being freed from our pain.

<u>We will allow others to express their feelings without interruption, interpretation or criticism.</u>

3. Care-taking vs. Care-giving — All of us have attempted to have our needs met by either plodding ahead without help (or blaming others for our failures) or by manipulating others to "help us" or "fix us." In the group, it is essential to resist the temptation to take responsibility for the rescue of others or to seek "guidance" from others in the group. If either strategy had worked before, we would not need the group process. Crosstalk is talking to another person about their problems rather than discussing your own problems. It is all right to refer briefly to what another person has said, but each of us needs to talk about our own experiences, feelings, and problems. For instance, "I felt scared when you talked about your relapse, because last week I had my own relapse (or problem)." We must be especially careful to avoid crosstalk which involves criticism, advice, or denial of another person's pain.

a. Criticism - If we feel criticized or judged, our response will be to stop sharing, and we will experience increased guilt, hopelessness and isolation. We need to be free to admit personal negative things, knowing that the response of the group will be loving acceptance. The only exception to the no criticism rule is when a member says or does something which violates the guidelines of this group. Such behavior is subject to discussion and group decision.

b. Advice -We tend to resist advice, often because it leaves us feeling talked down to. Sometimes we feel the advice is given without understanding or sympathy for the particulars of our personality, our history, or our situation. Even when we know the advice to be good, we may feel powerless to follow it. As a result, even good advice may leave us feeling hopeless. We are able to learn and grow from receiving love, support and acceptance and from seeking others getting well through the twelve steps. What we share here is not advice, but our own experience, strength and hope. <u>We will resist care-taking or seeking to be taken care of by group members.</u>

4. Honesty with kindness (speaking the truth in love) - As we express our feelings, it is important to be as honest as possible with ourselves and others. Where dishonesty is perceived in the group, confrontation may be necessary, but only after the person has been heard and acknowledged. Even someone in self-deception has his/her own right to the self-deceit. We will attempt to be open and honest, speaking the truth as we know it in love.

5. Self examination vs. blaming - Our goal is for our character to be transformed by the renewing of our minds (see Romans 12: 1-2). We must look at ourselves, not blaming others or projecting anger. This is not the same as placing responsibility for acts committed against us. <u>We must own responsibility for our own problems, not blaming others.</u>

6. Trust the process - Each meeting is designed, step by step, to set the stage for the healing power of God to touch and transform us. Each step we take is a move towards our healing and restoration. <u>We will trust each other and the group process to the best of our ability.</u>

7. Mutual accountability - The last thing the Lord has given to us for our growth is the church, the Body of Christ. Through the body, we can gain the sense of family and intimacy that we missed in our family of origin. <u>Therefore we must be accountable to one another.</u>

We can do by:

- Praying for each other daily.

- Being available in crisis.

- Loving enough to care and confront.

- Enjoying fellowship in a local church.

We will be mutually accountable to one another.

SIX DO'S AND DON'TS TO DEVELOP YOUR OWN SUPPORT SYSTEM

DO...

- Look for different qualities in different people.

- Accept and enjoy what people have to offer.

- Accept the limitations of others.

- Offer only what you are willing to give.

- Realize your time and friendships are precious.

- Keep trying.

DON'T...

- Expect any one person to answer all your needs in friendship.

- Expect people to give what they cannot or will not give.

- Expect others to respond exactly as you would.

- Try to be everyone's friend.

- Give up if you don't succeed immediately.

GROUP SUGGESTION FOR LEADERS OF *TWELVE STEP* GROUPS

You will want to adhere closely to the suggestions listed here in establishing and running your group. Doing so will enhance your success and effective ministry to others.

1. If you are running your group under church sponsorship (which is my suggestion), you will want to be sure of pastoral support. You may have to spend some time justifying the need to a skeptical (justifiably so) pastor. Let the pastor review the materials and answer any question he/she may have. Most pastors want to see growth occur in their sheep, and as long as you don't threaten him/her, their acceptance is fairly easy to obtain. Without their support, your group will have tough sledding, at best.

2. Allow at least four weeks between the initial announcement of the group and its actual beginning. This gives ample opportunity for recruitment, the purchase of books and supplies, etc. Once you get started, you don't want to have to stop because of logistical problems. To assist you, a Group Agreement, Sample Outreach Flyer and Sample Registration Form are available in Appendix 1-3.

3. Make sure you arrange for a room conducive for open discussion. A Sunday school room can be used, but a conference room with comfortable chairs is much preferred. Insure that it has adequate heating and air conditioning and a place for coffee and accessible restrooms.

4. The group should be arranged in a circle, with clear visibility for each member to see the others. Make sure there are no posts to hide behind.

5. Group size may vary, but I have found a minimum of six and a maximum of sixteen to be best. If you have more, it is better to run a second group. Since it is not necessary to be a trained professional group facilitator, though some group experience is definitely helpful, multiple groups are quite possible.

6. Your starting time should be the same each week, with a group closing time fifteen minutes after the start and a completion time of 1 1/2 to 2 hours. This helps build commitment from the group, as well as predictability and consistency which are desperate needs of all adults from dysfunctional families.

RULES FOR GROUP DISCUSSION

1. While others are talking, please let them finish without interruption.

2. No "fixing." We are to listen, support and be supported by one another — not give advice.

3. It's OK to feel angry here and to express your anger in the group. We will hear you, but try to be considerate of others in the room.

4. Speak in the "I" mode about how something or someone made you feel. Example: "I felt sad when..."

5. Keep sharing for no longer than five minutes in order that others in the group will also be able to share.

6. Try to share from the heart as honestly as you can. It's OK to cry, laugh, and be angry in the group without condemnation from others.

7. Remember that some people are here for the first time and others for the 60th time. Group members are in various stages of recovery. Give newcomers permission to be new and old-timers permission to be further along in their recovery. We are here to welcome everyone into our family and to help them feel safe about sharing their lives.

THE TWELVE STEPS

STEP ONE

"WE ADMIT WE WERE POWERLESS OVER ALCOHOL/ DRUG ABUSE AND COMPULSIVE BEHAVIOR — (OR

REACTION TO OUR LOSS) AND THAT OUR LIVES HAD
BECOME UNMANAGEABLE."

God's Word says in Romans 7:15, *"For what I am doing, I do not
understand; for I am not practicing what I would like to do, but I
am doing the very thing I hate."*

When we think about our behavior as being unmanageable, it can
be understood as a gross understatement. Most of us have had
tremendous struggles because of our dysfunctional families or
significant losses. As mentioned earlier in this book, most of us
suffer from various symptoms that make our lives difficult. The
most important step that we can go through in becoming full,
complete and whole, as God would have us become, is to fully
admit that we do not have any power within ourselves to overcome
that which has beset us. In Hebrews chapter 12, verses 1-2, it talks
about laying aside encumbrances and the weights and sins that do
so easily beset us. In order to do that we must be willing to admit,
"In and of myself I cannot accomplish the task." We must admit
our powerlessness and acknowledge the unmanageability of our
lives. We have now listed a few questions that would be helpful for
you to answer for yourself and be ready and willing to share with
your group on the second night of the *Twelve Step* program.

1. What makes me think my life has become unmanageable?

Describe, in detail, those areas of your life that seem to be beyond
your control to change.

2. What things have I tried in the past to overcome my
problem?

Have they worked? If not, why not?

3. What resources have I tried, if any, or people have I talked to trying to resolve the problems in my life?

4. Who have I depended upon and tried to manipulate or control in order to meet my needs?

It is vitally important that we acknowledge that without the power of the Lord Jesus Christ flowing within our lives, we cannot change. We know that Jesus is a change agent. He came to destroy the works of the devil and to heal all who were oppressed of the devil. Therefore we have a great hope. Although we cannot solve our problems ourselves, they can be solved when we admit our powerlessness and come to a place where we can turn our lives over to the Lord Jesus Christ.

"WE ADMIT WE WERE POWERLESS OVER ALCOHOL/ DRUG ABUSE AND COMPULSIVE BEHAVIOR — OR SIGNIFICANT LOSS AND THAT OUR LIVES HAD BECOME UNMANAGEABLE?'

God's Word says in Romans 7:15, *"For what I am doing, I do not understand; for I am not practicing what I would like to do, but I am doing the very thing I hate."*

STEP TWO

"WE CAME TO ACCEPT JESUS CHRIST AS OUR HIGHER POWER — BELIEVING HE COULD AND WOULD RESTORE US TO WHOLENESS'

Jesus said in Matthew 19:26, *"with men this is impossible; but with God all things are possible?"*

This scripture certainly speaks to the condition of most people who suffer great loss or are raised in a dysfunctional family system. How we have tried to resolve the problems in our lives! How we have tried to restore our own lives to wholeness! Yet, the truth of the matter is, it is only through the transformational power of the Lord Jesus Christ that true change will ever occur. It takes great faith to believe that we will ever become full and whole in God. Part of the transformation process covered in the books suggested is a belief that we are new creations in Christ at the moment we come to know Jesus. This step helps to reconfirm that we are, through the power of God, becoming greater than we ever thought we could. We have found a power greater than ourselves that can restore us. That power is the Lord Jesus Christ.

Let's now ask some questions. Write the answers for yourself as honestly as you can. Be willing and ready to share with your group.

1. When did I come to know Christ as my Savior?

Describe the circumstances, the setting and the initial experience.

2. What happened at the time that you came to know Christ? Describe it.

3. How long was it before you recognized that the initial experience did not seem to last, that the underlying problems were still there?

4. How have you tried to resolve this conflict within yourself? Do you believe that you just need more faith?

5. If Jesus really can restore us, why is it that it doesn't seem as though He has?

6. What must we do to become fully whole in Him?

This is a hard one, in that those of us who accepted Jesus Christ as our Lord and Savior have made an initial commitment to Him. The Bible indicates that, at the moment we come to know Christ, something truly miraculous happens. There is a new birth and a new creation occurs; yet, the old nature, which Paul talked about as "the sin that is within me," still tends to control our lives. This is why we must continue with the process of "working out our salvation with fear and trembling," and moving toward a place of wholeness in God. Our recovery takes time; it takes energy; it takes faith and an understanding of God's Word and His will for our lives. "Do not be weary in well doing, for in due season you will reap reward if you faint not." Keep believing that Jesus is restoring, do not give up. God really is on the throne and as you surrender more and more of yourself to Him; you will find that He will be able to change even the most despicable parts of your character.

"WE CAME TO ACCEPT JESUS CHRIST AS OUR HIGHER POWER — BELIEVING HE COULD AND WOULD RESTORE US TO WHOLENESS"

Jesus said in Matthew 19:26, *"With men this is impossible; but with God all things are possible."*

STEP THREE

"WE MADE THE DECISION TO TURN OUR WILL AND OUR LIFE OVER TO JESUS CHRIST"

Jesus said in Matthew 11:28-30, *"Come to Me, all who are weary and heavy-laden, and I will give you rest. ²⁹ Take My yoke upon you and learn from Me, for I am gentle and humble in heart, and YOU WILL FIND REST FOR YOUR SOULS. ³⁰ For My yoke is easy and My burden is light.". "*

Now we are coming to the crux of the matter. In reality, although we are born-again and Spirit-filled, there is still a part of us (usually our will, but sometimes our mind and emotions as well), that has yet to come under the Lordship of Christ. We must decide to fully turn our will and our life over to Jesus Christ. That is not a decision that can be made from the emotions, although many emotional appeals will bring you to the altar to do so. This is a decision that must be made from the will. Herein lays the major problem for most of us. Because of our loss of the family we were raised in, our will has become disabled. The ability to feel, to think, to trust, to decide has become disabled over time. Our lack of faith and confidence in ourselves leads to a lack of faith and confidence in the Lord. The inadequacies, inconsistencies, and instabilities of our family make it very difficult for us to make decisions and stick to them. If any of us could just "decide," wouldn't we have done it a long time before now? The surrender of our will and our lives to God takes a decision. We must have honesty, faith, and much prayer. As we do this, God by His Spirit will begin to transform us by the renewing of our minds. Don't miss this. Step three offers no compromise with reservation or delay. It calls for decision here and now. We are to surrender every part of ourselves to the Lord Jesus Christ for only He can truly restore us. We must recognize that we will ourselves to the Lord by faith. The important thing is not having a sense of that will power; it is being willing to practice it. We may not have all the understanding that we need, but what matters is the willingness to give our lives over to Jesus and that He will hear our prayers. He will answer, and He will help us as we are willing to turn our lives over to Him.

1.   Write down different ways and times that you have tried to surrender your will to the Lord.

What has been the effect?

2.   How long does that decision, usually emotionally based, last?

3.   If you were to give your life totally over to the Lord Jesus Christ, what do you think would change?

How do you feel about that? Be willing to share your feelings with the group as openly and vulnerably as you can.

4. Are you now willing to give your life over to the Lord Jesus Christ?

If you are, be willing to do so both privately and with someone you can trust as you covenant together to become more and more what God wants you to be.

Recognize that this is a decision that leads to many other decisions. With each decision that we make to surrender our will to the Lord Jesus Christ, we give a little bit of ourselves, but not the totality. We can only give what we know of ourselves. As we grow in God, more and more of our self, of our old nature, of our faults and failures, are revealed by the Holy Spirit. That is part of the job or responsibility of the Holy Spirit. You must be willing to surrender your life to the Lord and preferably to do so by, *"Therefore, confess your sins to one another, and pray for one another so that you may be healed. The effective prayer of a righteous man can accomplish much."* (James 5:16).

"WE MADE THE DECISION TO TURN OUR WILL AND OUR LIFE OVER TO JESUS CHRIST"

Jesus said in Matthew 11:28-30, *"Come to Me, all who are weary and heavy-laden, and I will give you rest. Take My yoke upon you and learn from Me, for I am gentle and humble in heart, and YOU WILL FIND REST FOR YOUR SOULS. For My yoke is easy and My burden is light."*

THE HEALING COMMUNITY

Steps four through nine deals with an aspect of the book *Journey to*

Wholeness called the healing community. This book discusses a process that we need to go through in the Body of Christ to insure that we become whole in God. This process is not an easy one. It is one that is clearly delineated in the Word and has been rediscovered by human behavioral specialists. It is most powerful in bringing about the transformation of our very characters. I encourage you to go through this with a sense of faith and awe because God will do something miraculous as you remain in the group and become honest with yourself and others. Further, for grief recovery, we must be willing to look at our lives before our loss as well as after and, allow the Lord to heal our inner most wounds.

STEP FOUR

"WE MADE A FEARLESS MORAL INVENTORY OF OUR HEART AND SOUL TO BETTER UNDERSTAND OURSELVES"

God's Word says in I John 1:8, *"If we say that we have no sin, we deceive ourselves, and the truth is not in us."*

For most people the fourth step is by far the most problematic. It is problematic in that you are asking the Holy Spirit to reveal the intentions and motivations of your heart. Jeremiah 17:9 says, *"The heart is more deceitful than all else, And is desperately sick; Who can understand it?"*

Verse 10 says that the Lord knows the heart. He understands the intentions of the heart. Further, Hebrews 4:12 tells us that the Word of God searches out the motivations and intentions of the heart. What we are working toward here is not just a change in behavior, but an internal change of our personality. This includes the surrender of self-centeredness; learning to practice honesty and humility, appreciation, forgiveness; promptness in forgiving wrongs and making amends; service to others; an example of a happy, positive life. All of us desire to have that and a step to doing that is to look honestly at the harmful characteristics of our own heart.

I do not believe that this needs to be done in an attempt to assassinate or condemn one's self. Romans 8:1 says, *"Therefore there is now no condemnation for those who are in Christ Jesus."* That includes self-condemnation, at which most of us are very good. There is no need to condemn yourself. You must look clearly at your own life and determine what areas need to change. In order to do this effectively, you must be willing to allow the Word of God to tell you what are the "rights" and what are the "wrongs" of your character. One way to do this is to read certain passages of scripture that deal with how we are to live before our fellow man. I would encourage you to read Matthew chapters 5 through 7, known as the Sermon on the Mount or the Beatitudes, and Galatians 5 which talks about the deeds of the flesh and the fruit of the Spirit. As you read these sections, be willing to write down and discuss in detail how you manifest certain characteristics in your everyday life. A very simple way to do this is to make a list of certain characteristics that must be worked on.

1. Do you have, as a part of your life, resentments that need to be changed?

[ ] Yes   [ ] No

List those people that you hold resentment against.

2. Have you ever been, or are you now, dishonest in relationships with yourself and others? Write it down. Be honest.

3. How have you allowed self pity to keep you in bondage and from seeking relationships and restoration in your life?

4. How have you allowed jealousy to creep into your life?

How has it manifested in relationships with others?

5. Do you ever allow yourself to become critical or intolerant of others?

If so, how do you do that?

6. Do you allow fear to rule your life?

List your main fears.

7. Do you have anger toward others?

How do you express it?

What have you tried to do to control it?

CHARACTER LIST

In the spaces below, list the character flaws that you bring to the Lord in faith, believing that the Lord will remove those flaws. In each case, write the flaw, how you feel about it, the underlying false belief or attitude you have about yourself because of the flaw and then the truth according to God's Word.

1. Flaw:_____

   Feeling: _____

   Belief: _____

   Truth:_____

2. Flaw: _____

   Feeling: _____

   Belief: _____

   Truth:_____

It is important to remember that none of us have perfect vision in our own lives. The reality is that we have blind spots. We are unable to fully look at all of our flaws. This is a defense mechanism that protects us from even greater harm. As you are doing an inventory of your life, you should not dig and probe trying to find every "jot and title" of problems. Bring this to the Lord asking the Holy Spirit to reveal any issues of false pride, resentment, jealousy, dishonesty, suspicion, criticism, intolerance, vindictiveness, self centeredness, etc., so that you can be prepared to do something with those characteristics.

"WE MADE A FEARLESS MORAL INVENTORY OF OUR HEART AND SOUL, TO BETTER UNDERSTAND OURSELVES"

God's Word says in I John 1:8, *"If we say that we have no sin, we deceive ourselves, and the truth is not in us."*

STEP FIVE

"WE CONFESSED TO GOD, TO OURSELVES AND TO ANOTHER HUMAN BEING THE EXACT NATURE OF OUR WRONGS (SINS)" (THIS INCLUDES OUR REAC-TION TO OUR LOSSES).

God's Word says in James 5:16 *"Therefore, confess your sins to one another, and pray for one another so that you may be healed. The effective prayer of a righteous man can accomplish much."*

It has been said that confession is good for the soul and is a primary part of the healing community. All of us must go through this process no matter how functional or dysfunctional our families may have been or how great our loss. It is the beginning of repentance in our lives. Here is where you want to confess, which means to tell your moral inventory to God and to at least one other human being. That one other human being can be a clergy member, pastor, counselor, sponsor, or someone else within your group. This is a very difficult thing to do, but it is tremendously cleansing. God promises healing as we confess and as we pray.

Confession alone brings a certain amount of relief but not total resolution. It takes prayer and believing God. The prayer of a person who knows Jesus and is walking in a right relationship with Him, avails much.

In this section, I want you to ask yourself the following questions:

1. Have I confessed all of my known sins, faults and negative characteristics to the Lord? How do I feel about this?

2. Have I confessed to at least one other human being?

If not, when will I do so? DATE: _____/_____/_____

I cannot reiterate how important this step is and yet, how difficult it is for most people to do. Many people who work Twelve Step programs come to this place and never finish. This is very unfortunate. Once you have gone through this, you will realize how easy it really was. The Lord Jesus Christ and those who listen to your moral inventory are ready to accept you just the way you are. God is a loving God. He is a gracious and good God. He is more than ready to forgive and forget all sin; to bury them in the sea of forgetfulness. Part of the next steps will be to assist you in forgiving yourself and those who have hurt you.

"WE CONFESSED TO GOD, TO OURSELVES AND TO ANOTHER HUMAN BEING THE EXACT NATURE OF OUR WRONGS (SINS)" (THIS INCLUDES OUR REACTION TO OUR LOSSES).

God's Word says in James 5:16, *"Therefore, confess your sins to one another, and pray for one another so that you may be healed. The effective prayer of a righteous man can accomplish much."*

STEP SIX

"WE BECAME ENTIRELY WILLING TO CHANGE AND ASKED GOD TO FORGIVE AND DELIVER US FROM OUR SINS"

Jesus said in Acts 3:19, *"Therefore repent and return, so that your sins may be wiped away, in order that times of refreshing may come from the presence of the Lord."*

This step is very important in that most of us are willing to lay our burdens down at the altar before the Lord, but we scoop them back up, put them on our backs and walk away from the altar with them. We must recognize that when God forgives, He forgets. We must learn that God will remove all of our character defects in His timing. We have been forgiven and delivered. The blood of Jesus Christ cleanses us from all sin - past, present, and future.

1. Have I allowed God to forgive me and deliver me from my sins?

2. In the past, how have I picked up my burdens and carried them with me?

Am I willing to now leave them with the Lord?

If so, what are my strategies for doing so?

4. How would I be different if I really believed I was forgiven?

Here is the beginning of a very humbling part of your twelve steps. We must be willing to accept the fact that we have a loving God who will receive us just the way we are. One of the things that we desperately needed as children growing up in dysfunctional families was a sense of love and acceptance. Here God is offering this to us, and the group is offering it as well. We must be willing to allow ourselves to be forgiven for our short comings. None of us are perfect. *"None are righteous, no not one."* All of us deserve God's punishment and yet, He offers mercy. What a marvelous God we serve! Allow God to do the work of forgiveness and to deliver you. I would make the serenity prayer my prayer everyday, *"God, grant me the serenity to change the things I can, accept the things I can't, and the wisdom to know the difference."* It is important to realize that one day at a time, God is changing us. Every day and in every way I am getting better and better by the grace of Almighty God.

"WE BECAME ENTIRELY WILLING TO CHANGE AND ASKED GOD TO FORGIVE AND DELIVER US FROM OUR SINS"

Jesus said in Acts 3:19, *"Therefore repent and return, so that your sins may be wiped away, in order that times of refreshing may come from the presence of the Lord."*

STEP SEVEN

"WE HUMBLY ASKED GOD, IN THE NAME OF JESUS, TO REMOVE OUR FAULTS"

God's Word says in James 4:6, *"But He gives a greater grace. Therefore it says, "GOD IS OPPOSED TO THE PROUD, BUT GIVES GRACE TO THE HUMBLE."*

After we have completed step five, humility has been experienced and self respect has been restored as a result of our admitting to God and to another human being the exact nature of our wrongs. Now we are suitably ready to carry through the provisions of steps six and seven. This brings us face to face with our real selves - the root of who we really are. In Isaiah, Jesus was described as a "root out of dry ground." Most of us can relate to that. We have no real source or substance as human beings. Truly, in and of ourselves we do not. Through the power of God's transformation, He can give us peace, restore our sanity and make us whole and complete in Him. In order to do this, we must humbly ask God in the name of Jesus, to remove our faults. Why would God want to do that for us? Have you ever asked yourself that question? Let's ask ourselves right now.

1.   Why would God want to remove my faults from me?

2.   Can God do it?

3.   Answer honestly before yourself. Are you willing to allow God to remove your faults?

4.   Are you willing to cooperate with God?

I would like to read several objectives of steps six and seven which come from The Little Red Book which talks about the Twelve Step program.

"THE SEVERAL OBJECTIVES" OF STEPS SIX AND SEVEN ARE:

1. To become honest and humble. To willingly seek God's help without reservation.

2. To perfect ourselves in the practice of unselfish prayer.

3. To be aware of our defective character traits.

4. To desire their removal.

5. To surrender completely all defects of character.

6. To believe that God can remove them.

7. To ask Him to take them all away.

I believe with all of my heart, that if you will submit to this process and ask God, you will receive. That asking, as recorded in the book of Matthew is, "keep on asking, keep on seeking, and keep on knocking." We ask God for help. We thank Him for recovery. We maintain our determination to grow in the things of God. There is nothing outstanding about the way you pray. It is the act of obedience and humility asking God to change you. He will give to you fully the fruit of the Holy Spirit. He will teach you to be cooperative, honest, tolerant, forgiving, and faithful and to have honest, unselfish love toward others.

"WE HUMBLY ASKED GOD, IN THE NAME OF JESUS, TO REMOVE OUR FAULTS?"

God's Word says in James 4:6, "God resisteth the proud, but giveth grace unto the humble?"

STEP EIGHT

"WE MADE A LIST OF ALL PERSONS WE HAD WRONGED AND BECAME WILLING TO MAKE AMENDS TO THEM ALL?"

Jesus said in Mark 11:25, *"And when ye stand praying, forgive, if ye have ought against any: that your Father also which is in*

Heaven may forgive you your trespasses."

Here is a way of practicing and/or working through our problems from our past. We must recognize that mistakes that we have made, sins that we have committed toward others, need to be corrected. We cannot always make amends for wrongs that we have done. We must be willing to do so as long as it will not cause greater harm to the person with whom we need to make amends.

1. Am I willing to make amends to people that I have wronged?

2. Make a list of all persons that you have wronged. The type of people that you might list includes:

a. Friends who you may have hurt verbally, nonverbally, or by not doing things promised.

b. Family members that you have hurt in the past.

c. Creditors.

d. The deceased -with this group we must bring our amends to the Lord and receive His forgiveness for the things that we have done wrong.

Place a number one (1) beside each name of those who are alive and available to be talked to about the wrongs that have been done. Place a number two (2) beside each name of those who are not available and/or it would cause greater harm to share with them and make amends than it would to keep silent.

I would strongly encourage you to share openly with the group and seek wise counsel before making amends to any individual. This is a form of maturity that is necessary in the making amends process.

   3.   What hindrances do I have to making amends with others?

It is very important that we make amends, make things right, in order to live in a right relationship with God. Once you have done so, there is no longer any fear of reprisal. That is a beautiful and exciting feeling — to be able to walk in a place where you can live and let live, knowing that there is little or no hurt feelings between you and another.

"WE MADE A LIST OF ALL PERSONS WE HAD WRONGED AND BECAME WILLING TO MAKE AMENDS TO THEM ALL?"

Jesus said in Mark 11:25, *"And when ye stand praying, forgive, if ye have ought against any: that your Father also which is in Heaven may forgive you your trespasses."*

STEP NINE

"WE MADE DIRECT AMENDS TO THOSE WE HAD WRONGED WHEREVER POSSIBLE, EXCEPT WHEN TO DO SO WOULD INJURE THEM OR OTHERS."

Jesus said in Matthew 5:9, *"Blessed are the peacemakers: for they shalt he called the children of God."*

Our goal is to make peace with people without bringing further harm. An example of this could be where you have said or done something behind their back and they do not know about it. To go and tell them about it could cause more harm to them than good. Those things should be confessed to the Lord and perhaps, to your sponsor or discussed in the group. Forgiveness needs to be received.

1. Have I made amends to those that I have hurt?

2. Who should I not make amends to? Why not?

3. What keeps me from following through on this important step?

THE COMPASSIONATE LIFE

Step ten begins the process of living out the compassionate life discussed in Journey to Wholeness. We will learn to live as fully and completely as possible the way Jesus did, lovingly reaching out to meet the needs of a lost and broken world. In terms of the grief process, we are moving towards acceptance of our loss and the re-embracing of life.

STEP TEN

"WE CONTINUE IN THE WAY OF THE LORD — REPENTING AND ASKING FOR HIS FORGIVENESS WHEN WE STUMBLE?"

God's Word said in I John 1:9, *"If we confess our sins, he is faithful and just to forgive us our sins, and to cleanse us from all unrighteousness."*

This is such a beautiful scripture. The reality of being human is that we all make mistakes. When we do, we must practice the process of putting off the old, renewing our mind and putting on the new. We must practice making things right with people. We must practice asking God for forgiveness and receiving that forgiveness without condemning ourselves. This is an ongoing lifestyle that must be developed.

1. Can you give an example of where you have stumbled and have/have not been through the process of repenting during this past week?

2. Is there someone that you are still harboring resentment, anger, or jealousy toward that you need to make things right with?

If so, when will you do so? DATE: _____/_____/_____

Discuss your feelings openly with the group.

"WE CONTINUE IN THE WAY OF THE LORD — REPEATING AND ASKING FOR HIS FORGIVENESS WHEN WE STUMBLE?"

God's Word said in I John 1:9, *"If we confess our sins, he is faithful and just to forgive us our sins, and to cleanse us from all unrighteousness."*

STEP ELEVEN

"WE SEEK GOD'S WILL FOR OUR LIVES DAILY THROUGH PRAYER AND THE READING OF HIS WORD — PRAYING FOR THE POWER OF HIS HOLY SPIRIT IN ORDER TO WALK CLOSELY WITH HIM."

God's Word said in Philippians 4:6-7, *"Be anxious for nothing, but in everything by prayer and supplication with thanksgiving let your requests be made known to God. And the peace of God, which surpasses all comprehension, will guard your hearts and your minds in Christ Jesus."*

Every individual believer must be willing to give away their own life. In order to do so, to live out a compassionate life, you must be strengthened daily by prayer and the reading of God's Word. It is amazing to note how many pastors do not spend private time continuing to develop that intimate relationship with the Lord Jesus Christ. This is the foundation for everything we do. It is not our relationship in the church; it is not our service for the Lord. He can live without that. What He wants is intimate fellowship with us. We must be willing to walk closely with Him by the leading of the Holy Spirit.

    1. Have you developed a daily devotional life?

        [ ] Yes   [ ] No

If not, why not?

    2. What could you do to develop your devotional life?

    3. Ask of the group how they function in this area. Covenant with one another to develop the intimate relationship by daily reading and prayer.

188

I cannot emphasize enough the importance of keeping your hearts and minds through Jesus Christ. The devil is constantly attacking us, especially those of us raised in dysfunctional families. Self-pity is often the door through which he attacks the grieving. It is vital that we keep a close relationship with the Lord and with one another. It is important to be vulnerable with each other, to be willing to confess faults and to lay your life open before the Lord and others that you can trust.

"WE SEEK GOD'S WILL FOR OUR LIVES DAILY THROUGH PRAYER AND THE READING OF HIS WORD — PRAYING FOR THE POWER OF HIS HOLY SPIRIT IN ORDER TO WALK CLOSELY WITH HIM"

God's Word said in Philippians 4:6-7, *"Be anxious for nothing, but in everything by prayer and supplication with thanksgiving let your requests be made known to God. And the peace of God, which surpasses all comprehension, will guard your hearts and your minds in Christ Jesus."*

STEP TWELVE

"WE HAVE BECOME NEW CREATURES IN CHRIST — FREE OF ABUSIVE AND COMPULSIVE BEHAVIOR, OVERCOMING OUR LOSSES- AND WE SEEK TO CARRY THE GOOD NEWS OF CHRIST AND THE PRINCIPLES OF RESTORATION TO OTHERS, AS WE CONTINUE TO LIVE BY THESE STEPS."

Jesus said in Mark 5:19, *"And He did not let him, but He said to him, " Go home to your people and report to them what great things the Lord has done for you, and how He had mercy on you."*

This is such an interesting statement. It is both a truth and a becoming truth. All of us are free. Jesus has made us free. Yet we are becoming freer all the time as we continue through our Twelve Step process. As we continue in our relationship with the Lord, reading His Word, praying, worshipping, witnessing, we grow more in Him. There is a responsibility that we have to carry the good news of Christ, the power that He has to restore lives and to live that life before others. That is really our testimony. Revelation 12:11 says "*And they overcame him because of the blood of the Lamb and because of the word of their testimony, and they did not love their life even when faced with death.*" What a beautiful verse of scripture. All of us are truly more than conquerors in Christ Jesus. To live that conquering life we must daily submit our lives and admit our helplessness. We must daily confess our faults. We must daily read the Word. We must daily walk in the light of these twelve steps. As we do, God will continue to work out all of the garbage in our lives.

We will grow more and more faithful in Him. It is very, very important that we continue to live according to these steps and the principles outlined in the Word of God. As we do so, God will pour out His blessings upon us.

1.   When was the last time I shared my faith in the Lord Jesus Christ?

2.   What keeps me from witnessing?

3.   What might I do to reach out to those in my community?

I am willing, and I have made a strategy to reach out to someone in my world with the gospel of Jesus Christ. I trust that all of you will do that because I know that there is no greater relationship than the relationship that we can have with Jesus Christ along with an honest relationship with one another as brothers and sisters in the Body of Christ.

"WE HAVE BECOME NEW CREATURES IN CHRIST — FREE OF ABUSIVE AND COMPULSIVE BEHAVIOR OVERCOMING OUR LOSSES- AND WE SEEK TO CARRY THE GOOD NEWS OF CHRIST AND THE PRINCIPLES OF RESTORATION TO OTHERS, AS WE CONTINUE TO LIVE BY THESE STEPS."

Jesus said in Mark 5:19, *"And He did not let him, but He said to him, " Go home to your people and report to them what great things the Lord has done for you, and how He had mercy on you."*

CONCLUSION

If you have just gone through this program, through all Twelve Steps, you have most likely solved many problem areas in your life. However, you will also recognize that you are not yet complete and whole, but that you are moving in that direction. As you continue to practice these things with the Lord and with others, you will find that you will grow daily in the ways of God. Once you have been through the process the first time, the majority of things that need to change have been done by the power of the Holy Spirit. We must choose to believe and receive His forgiveness, restoration, and healing and to practice those things that we have learned.

I trust that you will continue to grow and support your local church and be more involved in reaching out to those who hurt, living out the compassionate lifestyle in accordance with the will of the Lord.

"Like apples of gold in settings of silver Is a word spoken in right circumstances".
Proverbs 25:11

CHAPTER 8:

EVALUATING GROUPS

In the preceding chapters, it was suggested that the members of the group should set some personal goals for their group experience. It is possible that many of the goals may not be attainable within the time frame of the group. If a member sets as a personal goal to become a fully self-actualizing person, in the terms of Maslow's Model of Personality (1962), it may be necessary for the leader to suggest a more realistic goal. A realistic goal must be one that is attainable within the time limits of the group. The other side of the question is the possibility of setting goals that are too limited in scope. Again, the leader must help the members set goals that will bring a sense of achievement to the members.

Some of the goals that members will wish to accomplish may only be evaluated subjectively, that is, in the opinion of the member himself. Other objectives or goals can be evaluated objectively. Some of the areas that may be subjectively evaluated are:

Sensitivity: Smith (1966) defines sensitivity as the ability to predict what an individual will feel, say, and do about you, himself, and others. Sensitivity is that ability to sense what other people will think or feel. Smith defines the components of sensitivity as follows:

1. The general tendency to make favorable or unfavorable evaluations of others.

2. The variability a person introduces into his estimation of others.

3. The amount of accurate empathy a person feels and can communicate.

4. The accuracy of observation.

5. The ability to build accurate stereotypes.

6. Having a working model of personality traits.

Sensitivity, although it is more of a subjective determination, can also be evaluated by the trained leader to a considerable extent. Smith believes that these components can be taught and measured. In the group situation, not only can the leader evaluate an individual's growth in sensitivity, but the other members can also evaluate that growth or lack thereof. It can be expected that a certain amount of sensitivity will be learned through participation in the group.

The leader can help facilitate sensitivity training by his or her responses to the members during a group sessions.

Anxiety level: Some of the members of the group may have a history of chronic anxiety that has followed them for years. These members would most certainly experience an increased level of anxiety at the beginning of the group sessions. It is one of the goals of the group to help these members conquer at least some of that anxiety. Again, this goal may be primarily a subjective evaluation, but it is also possible for the leader and the other members of the group to see and evaluate the difference in any manifested signs of anxiety in members as the group progresses.

OBJECTIVIE MEASUREMENT OF GROUP SUCCESS

The objective measurement of a group's success or growth depends on how clearly and precisely the goals of the group were set. Most of the test instruments that are available have met with considerable problems concerning their validity because of the self-reporting aspect of the instrument. Notwithstanding, some significant information may be obtained through the use of these instruments. Bates (1968) insists that achievable goals can be specific, can be met, and can be measured.

Following are some of the assessment tools that are available. The reader is encouraged to consult the bibliography for the source of these instruments. Some of the following information was taken from Bates and Johnson (1972). The group counselor should have this very valuable book in their personal library for instant reference to many areas of group leadership.

Allport Vernon Lindzey. *Study of Values* **(1960)**
This is a widely known scale for measuring dominant values in personality. The instrument has been widely researched and found to be reasonably valid. This before and after instrument, should be used with caution as the six measured values are not independent of one another and therefore statistical techniques must be used with care.

Bills, Robert E. Index of Adjustment and Values.
This is an excellent instrument for measuring changes in self-concept, both in relation to self and to perceptions of others. This is an easy to score test and has forms for elementary, junior high school, high school, and adult levels. The reliability and validity of this instrument of measurement have been established by considerable research. The reader may write to Robert E. Bills, School of Education, University of Alabama, for the instrument and manual, specifying the age level to be measured.

Coopersmith, Stanley. Self-Esteem Inventory. (1926-1979)
This inventory is directed toward children and is intended to measure an individual's general appraisal of his worth, which Coopersmith claims remains rather stable over a period of several years. He also posits that people are reluctant to accept evidence that they are better or worse than they themselves have decided. This fifty-item inventory and the accompanying scales, sort the items into two groups — those indicative of high self-esteem and those indicative of low self-esteem.

Because self-esteem or the lack thereof, plays such an important role in a person's relationships with others, groups for younger people can be very constructive in the Christian community Unfortunately, some of the misguided teachings of the Christian concepts of humility have been interpreted as meaning that a person should not think well of himself. Information about the SEI may be obtained from www.mindgarden.com/products/cseis/htm.

O'Sullivan, M. et. al. (1965).

This measurement tool consists of a series of booklets which group leaders might use to measure the components of sensitivity. The tool is similar to the method suggested by Smith (1966). The authors present pictures which depict relationships in a variety of ways. The material contains no written material and thus is non-verbal. The booklets may be obtained from the Sheridan Supply Co., Beverly Hills, California.

Petrus, W. PAC Index of Maturity.

This instrument is based on the Eric Berne (1961) parent-adult-child model of personality. It uses the Q-methodology in a measure of maturity. The instrument is designed to measure any movement toward "maturity" (as defined by PAC) which occurs as a result of group experience. The tools are intended primarily for adolescents. Copies of this instrument may be obtained from Bates and Johnson (1972).

Rotter, Julian B. (1950) Incomplete Sentence Blank.

This is a semi-projective tool which generates a quantitative score. The score, according to the author of the test, may serve as an index of maladjustment. It can therefore be used as a screening instrument, and as a pre and post measure of the growth in the group.

Copies of the instrument together with a scoring manual may be obtained from PEARSON, 19500 Bulverde Road, San Antonio, TX 78259-3701 or www.psychcorp.pearsonsassessments.com /pai/ca.

Shultz, William, FIRO-B and FIRO-F

The FIRO-B stands for Fundamental Interpersonal Relations Orientation Behavior, and the purpose of the test is to measure how an individual characteristically relates to others. Shultz suggests that people have three interpersonal needs areas which involve joy and misery inclusion, control, and affection. The instrument leads to six scores: expressed inclusion and wanted inclusion behavior, expressed control and wanted control behavior, expressed affection and wanted affection behavior. In measuring "Affection" the FIRO-B includes a statement. "I act close and personal toward people," to measure expressed affection behavior, and "I want people to get close and personal with me" to measure wanted affection behavior.

The FIRO-F stands for Fundamental Interpersonal Relations Orientation Feelings and is designed to measure an individual's characteristic feelings toward others. The factors of the test are significance, competence, and lovability. The instrument measures interaction as well as individual traits. Bates and Johnson (1972) suggest that this test may be used with children and adults.

Shostrom, Everett L. P01, Personal Orientation Inventory.
This measure is based on Maslow's Self-Actualizing constructs. The respondent is to pick one of the each of the 150 pairs of statements that consistently applies to himself on a separate answer sheet. A profile sheet is generated which provides scores on a variety of dimensions such as self-actualizing value, spontaneity, self-regard, acceptance of aggression, capacity for intimate contact, etc. The reader may contact Everett L. Shostrom, through the Educational and Industrial Testing Service, San Diego, California 92107.

Tyler, Leona E. Vocational Choice Cards.
These cards consist of a set of small (1"X 3") cards on which are typed fifty occupations which were chosen by one group of students as those vocations which most interested them. The student is asked to place each card into one of three categories: "Would choose." "Would Not Choose" and "No Opinion." The measure is suitable for group administration and serves as a useful measure of the degree to which students' vocational horizons have expanded as a result of group counseling. This measure would not be used in a Christian Growth Group unless the group was designed to help young people in a church setting to discover

vocational preferences as a result of the group counseling.

In some groups, the leader may feel that there have been no group goals set, only individual goals. In this case, measurement of the group's success must be done on an individual basis. There are many other tests and measures that are available. The reader is referred to any college library for further research. Occasionally, one of the designed group programs will include a measure of group effectiveness.

Although most of the tests that were mentioned for use in screening and for a basis of group discussions in an earlier chapter are not designed as pre and post testing instruments, they may serve to shed some light on any changes that may have taken place in members of the group during the group experience.

Even if the leader decides not to use a formalized instrument to measure the effectiveness of the group, it is important that the group and the leader together evaluate and be allowed to share their feelings about the entire group experience. This may best be done during the last session of the group.

Some group leaders find that follow-up contacts with the members of a group experience can produce evidence of continued growth or lack of growth. The object of counseling, whether personal or group, is to produce change for the better in feelings, beliefs, and behavior. In the Christian Growth Group, the goal is to help individual members become more successful in their Christian walk, in their relationships with other members in the Body of Christ, and in their relationships with other people in general. These goals may be tested without too much trouble if the members of the group are a part of the same or closely related Christian communities. The pastor or elders of the community will be able to provide some valuable insights into the changes that have occurred in the members who attended a group.

The group leaders may elect to construct their own test of efficiency. The test constructed by the leader(s) may not meet all of the standards of validity and reliability required of a good scientific test, but these tests can answer some important questions for the leadership that will help them in planning other groups in the future. The leaders of a small group must not be afraid to face the possible criticism of members of the group. The test or questionnaire should be done anonymously to insure, as much as possible, honest answers. Some of the questions that the questionnaire might include are:

1. Was the group helpful to you personally? What could have been done to make the group more helpful?

2. On a scale of one to ten (one being the lowest in effectiveness and ten being the highest level of effectiveness) rate each of the leaders of the group.

3. How would you describe the leadership style of the leader? The co-leader?

4. Were certain members of the group allowed too much opportunity to dominate the sessions?

5. Would you consider another group conducted by the same leadership? By another leader?

As a matter of fact, it is always advisable for the leader of Christian Growth Groups in a Christian Community to consult the pastor or elders of the community for their input as to any growth that they have been able to observe. Not only is this a good way to evaluate the group experience, but it also lets the pastor and elders know that the purpose and goals of Christian Growth Groups are of the highest Christian intentions. It is important to note again at this point the importance of confidentiality. In seeking input from the leadership of the church or fellowship, the group leader must never compromise his commitment to the group as far as confidentiality is concerned.

On a higher level than has already been suggested, there is a need for Christian counselors to become interested in the field of research in the area of Christian Growth Groups. This activity is usually considered a part of a doctoral project, but the information about evaluations and methods used should be gathered long before the student begins the doctoral level. Not nearly enough work has been done and documented in the area of the possibilities for Christian Growth Groups in dealing with problems that plague the Christian community — problems such as spousal, child, and elder abuse; drug and alcohol addiction; sexual orientation, and on and on.

POSSIBLE MISUSE OF GROUP

As in any endeavor where people are involved, there are possibilities of misuse. This is especially true in the small group because of the possibility of the wrong kind of leadership. It has been demonstrated that groups can affect much good in the Christian community and in the community at large, but they can be nurturing or toxic in the same way that a church can be nurturing or toxic. Groups can cause harm by encouraging people to engage in nonfunctional behavior patterns. Bates and Johnson (1972) warn that small groups are not to be thought of as "a harmless toy which can be manipulated freely with no fear of negative consequences." Bates and Johnson further offer in the Appendix B of their book a suggestion for specific minimum training standards for leaders of various types of groups. Some of the dangers noted by Bates and Johnson include:

When a leader of a group does not recognize or accept the responsibility for the group there is evidence of ill-prepared leaders. In these groups the privacy of the members may be invaded or they may find themselves overpowered by a dictatorial style of leadership.

Professional groupers often consider themselves as experts and use their many hours in groups as an opportunity to manipulate less experienced members. Without the protection of a well-trained leader, this manipulation will lead to a toxic result in the other members.

There have been many cases where perennial groupers have used the small group situation as a sexual mating ground, apparently never quite grasping the concept that the group is relevant only as it enables members to live richer lives outside the weekly interaction experienced.

A group leader with a high level of personal assertive behavior and who misuses that behavior may do considerable damage to group members.

Groups have come under severe attack, and the experiences of groups led by irresponsible, incompetent "leaders" have made many of these justifiable attacks. Gary Allen (1968) in his classic work entitled, Hate Therapy is basically an attack on irresponsible group leadership. There is growing favor for Certification of Competency for those who do groups.

In any group situation where there may be a high level of emotions exchanged, there is always a possibility of the wrong kinds of emotional interaction between people in the group. The leader must be on the alert to prevent any unhealthy exchange, whether sexual or simply physical in nature. As noted above, groupies often go from one group to another in search of a sexual encounter with some emotionally unstable individual, but even relatively normal people can be seduced in a moment of weakness where there is a great deal of understanding and love being manifested. The wife who has spent many years with an uncaring, cold husband can be "swept off of her feet" by a caring man in the group. Teenagers are particularly vulnerable in the group situation.

I was facilitating a group for teens at the university one weekend. The teens were to meet on Friday evening for four hours and then go home for the night to return on Saturday. When the groups were dismissed, some of the boys and girls hid behind one of the portable classrooms that we were using for the sessions. After all of the adults left, they returned to one of the classrooms and spent the night. In the early hours of the morning some very troubled parents came looking for their children. The University was very embarrassed as were the organizers of the encounter weekend.

Some provision should have been made to make sure all of the teens actually left the University campus. Fortunately, there were no lawsuits.

The emotional level of teenagers is extremely volatile. The leader must always be alert to the possibility of an eruption of emotions that might result in physical violence.

The leader of the group must guard against the possibility of violence in forcing the wrong kinds of feelings and ideas in the group. It may be obvious to everyone in the group that a person (or a couple) is in what would be considered an impossible marriage, but in the process of the group, every effort must be made to avoid any suggestion that the marriage should be dissolved. It is possible to refer the couple to individual counseling, but no advice can be allowed in the group situation regarding the final outcome of the marriage.

There is always the possibility of a leader, with many unresolved issues of his own, forming a group and using the group as a place to exploit those issues. A leader with unresolved hostility toward women will not make a good group leader. Group facilitators, like any other Christian counselor, must first resolve their own issues, or at least be in the process of resolving them, before taking on the responsibility of trying to guide a group to healing. It is the old splinter or mote in the eye story that must be kept in mind here.

Without a doubt, the most heinous and criminal use of Group Dynamics would be the brain washing activities of the communist world during the period after World War II and up to the present. During the Korean and Vietnam conflicts, many American soldiers were captured and systematically "brain washed" into believing that America was the real enemy. After the Korean conflict settled down, a number of American military men chose to remain in Korea as their chosen homeland.

The brain washing technique was usually done in small group settings. The participants were forced to listen to many hours of communist propaganda while they were deprived of food and water. A very strange dynamic occurred that baffled the experts. These American personnel often began to relate to their tormentors and to believe the communist's lies. It can be reasonably assumed that a great number of the victims experienced years of "flash backs" and had considerable trouble adjusting to life back in the home environment.

In the seamy underworld of espionage, counterintelligence, and international secret spy activity, this unconscionable activity still is used to control large segments of a population. The Nazis in Germany used the group technique to move almost the entire nation into believing that the atrocities against the Jews either did not happen or were completely justified.

Group Dynamics, whether in small or very large groups, can become a powerful weapon in controlling the thoughts and actions of people. A considerable amount of research has been done in the field of sociology on the effects of a group, any group, on the behaviors of people.

In the deep South, one can find a history of groups of white men who were able to convince themselves and others that the black man was evil. These otherwise reasonably good citizens were capable of hanging, flogging, and burning blacks without any noticeable remorse.

The Klu Klux Klan was responsible for the torture and death of many black people, because the nature of the KKK had a powerful "brain washing" influence on certain members of the community.

As noted in the early part of this text, "Good groups can be very good, and bad groups can be horrendous!" As is the case with ministry of any kind, it can be nourishing or toxic. Toxic parents, toxic churches, and toxic groups can cause more emotional problems than can be imagined. A toxic ministry or a toxic group (family) is characterized by some common elements.

1. Inadequate leaders are simply not aware of their toxic affect or their lack of leadership. The individual who thinks that all

there is to leading a group is gathering together a group of people and having them share their problems, is doomed to cause great confusion in the minds of some of the members in the group. Fortunately, most people who enter groups are not so vulnerable as to suffer permanent damage. An individual who has had even a little education in the field of psychology will be able to detect inadequacies in the leadership from the beginning. The person who has had some training in counseling, and especially group counseling, will fare even better. It is a small group of people who will be damaged most (indeed, may have already been damaged by toxic parent. or toxic church leadership). These people are those who are in greatest need of help from the group but experience some of the same harmful experiences that they suffered in other situations with inadequate leadership.

2. "The most flagrant misusers of groups are ill-prepared group leaders who apparently do not recognize that accepting responsibility for a group implies an ethical commitment to its members to insure that they experience positive growth, that they find caring relationships, that they can place trust in the leadership, that their personal privacy will not be invaded, and that they find the process manipulated, not themselves" (Bates and Johnson, 1972, page 187).

3. The expert is the professional grouper who has "clocked in so many hours in groups" that he or she has become less interested in the needs of the members than in the process of the group. These are the leaders who will become angry and accusatory towards members of the group if things do not "go as they should," They will not in any way accept any responsibility for problems that may develop in a group.

4. The professional grouper is the person who has participated in so many groups that he or she has become the "expert" in matters of conducting the group. They will often disagree with the leader or even attempt to usurp the authority of the leader. This situation demands strong, yet wise actions by the leader or leaders in the case of co-leadership. In co-leadership, it is imperative that

the leaders stand together in the handling of the professional grouper in order to limit the amount of damage done to the inexperienced members. There will be times in groups when an individual may be more highly trained than either the leader or the co-leader. However, ethics and common sense indicate that the more expert individual must be in submission to the appointed leadership of the group.

5. The perennial groupers represent those individuals who use the group experience as sexual hunting grounds. It is not that these individuals are always aware of their problem, but they have discovered that groups often have members in them who are love starved and will welcome the comfort and care (although the care is completely of a selfish nature). The greater tragedy is when the leader is the one who is using the group to seek and find individuals to use to satisfy his own sexual needs (or more correctly sexual wants). The harm that can be done to unsuspecting young females (or males) is so devastating as to require years of psychological counseling.

6. Leadership with unresolved emotional issues can almost subconsciously react in a hostile manner to members of the group who "rub them the wrong way" so as to touch a raw nerve of the unresolved issues.

Bates and Johnson (1972) suggest ways to avoid getting into a toxic group. These seven suggestions are presented here as ways that a leader may avoid generating a group that may become toxic, or at least mildly damaging to some of the unsuspecting members.

1. The forming of a new group should not be advertised in the newspaper. It is unethical first of all and also allows for the professional grouper to "sign-up." Membership in a group is best selected by referrals from pastors, Christian counselors and secular counselors. There may be times when a referral from a government agency is acceptable in view of the fact that the referee is usually well-known to the agency and will be under the direct supervision of the referral agency.

2. Groups of less that six or more than sixteen can precipitate such problems as scapegoating and ganging-up. As noted earlier in the chapter on ways of organizing a group, twelve to thirteen is the ideal number. It is interesting to note that even though this "ideal" number was not suggested by a Christian counselor, it is the number that comprised the group that made up the inner circle of disciples that followed Jesus Christ (12).

3. Members should not be permitted to join a group on impulse. The leadership of a group should help perspective members take time to think and pray about joining a group. The person who is in desperate need of immediate emotional help would most likely receive more help from a one on one counseling experience. Impulse joiners may expect too much, too soon from the group.

4. Although some groups are designed to help close associates become more sensitive and understanding of the needs of their fellow workers, it is unwise to have close associates participate in an encounter group where deep emotional feeling may be shared.

5. Those who run groups should not attempt to impress prospective members by lavish surroundings. Good groups can happen anywhere. The meeting place should be clean, comfortable, accessible and reasonably secure to insure the confidentiality of the group, but beyond those simple needs, the surroundings should not be distractive.

6. A group should never be allowed to develop into a place to share racial, cultural, sexual or intellectual prejudices.

Groups should never be conducted without the proper accountability. Leaders of groups should always be under the headship of spiritual leadership. It is also very wise to have a licensed professional on call, who can be called upon or consulted in cases beyond the training level of the group leader(s). A group leader, like other professionals in the counseling field, is accountable to the laws of the state in which they practice. Malpractice law suits are becoming more and more prevalent.

Having the right kind of insurance and legal advice can save the group leader considerable grief while preventing toxic damage from occurring in individual members of the group.

BIBLIOGRAPHY

Allport, Gorden; Vernon, Philip E.; and Lidzey, Gardner. (1960). Study of Values, 3rd edition. Boston: Houghton Miffin.

Back, K, (1982), Beyond Words, NY.: Sage.

Bates, Marilyn M, and Johnson, Clarence D, (1972), Group Leadership: A Manual for Group Counseling Leadership. Denver: Love Publishing Company.

Bates, Marilyn. A Test of Group Counseling. Personnel and Guidance Journal, April, 1968.

Berne, Eric, (1961). Transactional Analysis. New York: Grove Press.

Bonner, Hubert. (1959), Group Dynamics: Principles and Applications. New York: The Ronald Press Company.

Dibbert, Michael T, and Wichern, Frank B. (1985), Growth Groups: A Key to Christian Fellowship, and Spiritual Maturity in the Church. Grand Rapids: Zondervan.

Durkheim, Emile, (1898), Representations Individuals et Representations Collectives, Rev. De Met, et de Mor, 6 274-302.

Friedman, William H, (1994), How to Do Groups, 2nd Edition. Northvale: Jason Aronson, Inc.

Griffin, Em. (1982), Getting Together Downer Grove: InterVarsity Press, Hartman, 1. (1987). Five Audiences. Nashville: Abington.

Kaplan, Harold I, and Sadock, Benjamin J, (1993), Comprehensive Group, Psychotherapy, 3rd edition, Baltimore: Williams and Wilkins,

Klein, Robert H., Bernard, Harold S., Singer, David L. (1992), Handbook of Contemporary Group Psychotherapy: Contribution from Object Relations, Self Psychology and Social Systems Theories, Madison: International Varsity Press.

Luft, Joseph and Ingram, Harry. (1963) The Johari Window, A Graphic Model of Awareness in Interpersonal Relations. In Group Processes: An Introduction to Group Dynamics. By Joseph Luft, Palo Alto: National Press Books.

Maslow, Abraham H, (1962), Toward a Psychology of Being 2nd Ed, New York: Van Nostrand Reinhold.

Mehrabian, A, Communication Without Words, Psychology Today. Vol. 2. 1968. pp. 52-55.

Meier, Paul D., Minieth, Frank B., Wichern, Frank B, and Ratcliff, Donald E, (1991). Introduction to Psychology and Counseling: Christian Perspectives and Applications, 2nd Edition, Grand Rapids: Baker Book Company.

Ohlson, Merle M, (1977), Group Counseling, 2nd Edition, New York: Holt, Rinehart and Winston,

Otto, Herbert A, (1970) Group Methods to Actualize Human Potential. Beverly Hills: The Holistic Press.

Peck, M. Scott, (1978). The Road Less Traveled, New York: Simon and Schuster.

Pettus, William F, (1970), PAC: An Instrument Designed to Provide an Operational Definition of Maturity Based on Berne's model of Personality.

Rogers, Carl, (1970), Carl Rogers on Encounter Groups. NY, Harper Row.

Shaffer, J.B.P. and Galinsky, M.D. (1974), Models of Group Therapy and Sensitivity Training. Englewood Cliffs, N.J.: Prentice Hall.

Schultz, William, (1958). The FIRO Scales. Consulting Psychologists Press, 577 College Ave. Palo Alto, California 94301.

Shaw, M.E, (1981), Group Dynamics, 3rd Edition, NY. McGraw Hill,

Shostrom, Everett I, P01, Personal Orientation Inventory

Educational and Industrial Testing Service, San Diego, CA 92107.

Smith, Henry Clay. (1966). Sensitivity to People. New York: McGraw-Hill, Tyler, Leona E, (1964). Vocational Choice Cards. University of Oregon, Eugene, Ore.

Winters, Walter, (1966). Perception of Self Unpublished inventory, Huntington Beach, California.

Wuthnow, Robert. (1994). Sharing the Journey: Support Groups and America's New Quest for Community. New York: Maxwell Macmillian International.

Yalom, Irvin D, (1969). The Theory and Practice of Group Psychotherapy New York: Basic Books.

Zimpfer, David G, (1969), Group Procedures in Guidance: A Bibliography Albany, N.Y.: New York State Personnel & Guidance Association.

THE TEACHING MINISTRY OF DR. STAN DEKOVEN

Dr. DeKoven conducts seminars nationally and internationally based on his books in Practical Christian Living. He is available for limited engagements for church seminars, retreats and conferences.

For a complete listing of topics and books, contact:

Dr. Stan DeKoven, President
Walk in Wisdom Seminars
1115 D Street
Ramona, CA 92065
(760) 789-4700
1-800-9 VISION

Other Books by Dr. DeKoven on similar topics:

Grief Relief
Journey to Wholeness: Restoration of the Soul
40 Days to the Promise: A Way Through the Wilderness
Marriage and Family Life: A Christian Perspective
Turning Points: Ministry in Crisis
On Belay! Introduction to Christian Counseling
Family Violence: Patterns of Destruction
The Healing Community
Substance Abuse

To purchase, contact Vision Publishing at
www.booksbyvision.com

APPENDIX 1:

GROUP AGREEMENT

1. I agree to keep all communication and identities anonymous and confidential.

2. I will allow others to express their feelings without interruption, interpretation, or criticism.

3. I will resist care-taking or seeking to be taken care of by group members.

4. I will attempt to be open and honest, speaking the truth as I know it, in love.

5. I will own responsibility for my own problems and not blame others.

6. I will trust the members of the group and the group process, to the best of my ability.

7. I will be accountable to the members of the group and, the other members of the group will be accountable to me and each other.

Signed:_____

Witness:_____

Date:_____

APPENDIX 2:

SAMPLE OUTREACH FLYER

CHRISTIAN GROWTH GROUP AT
FAMILY CARE CENTER

BEGINNING TUESDAY EVENING
FROM 6:30 - 8:00 P.M.

WITH DR. STAN E. DEKOVEN

- Participants will learn and practice discipleship and healing for broken relationships and past hurts.

- Learn to listen to others and respond with compassion.

- Offer and receive support and assistance in a safe, confidential environment while building new relationships.

- Work through conflicts in a Christian fashion (Ephesians 4:25-5:2).

- Learn to grow towards maturity in Christ as we move through life's transitions.

- The purpose of the Family Care Center is to assist individuals, families and groups to become all that God has created them to be. It is only through Jesus that we can become whole. He uses members of the Body of believers, the Church, to help in that process.

For More Information Call:
Dr. Stan E. DeKoven
Ramona, CA 92065
(760) 789-4700

A Program of The Family Care Services

APPENDIX 3:

SAMPLE REGISTRATION FORM

REGISTRATION FOR TWELVE STEP PROGRAM

Name:_____

Address:_____

City, State Zip:_____

Type of Family Dysfunction:
- Alcohol
- Drugs
- Abuse
- Grief/Loss

Other:_____

Present Compulsion:
- Work
- Fear
- Eating
- Anger
- Sex
- Drugs

Other:_____